GUYANA
in Pictures

Karen Sirvaitis

Clifton Park - Halfmoon Public Library
475 Moe Road
Clifton Park, New York 12065

Twenty-First Century Books

Contents

Lerner Publishing Group, Inc. realizes that current information and statistics quickly become out of date. To extend the usefulness of the Visual Geography Series, we developed www.vgsbooks.com, a website offering links to up-to-date information, as well as in-depth material, on a wide variety of subjects. All of the websites listed on www.vgsbooks.com have been carefully selected by researchers at Lerner Publishing Group, Inc. However, Lerner Publishing Group, Inc. is not responsible for the accuracy or suitability of the material on any website other than www.lernerbooks.com. It is recommended that students using the Internet be supervised by a parent or teacher. Links on www.vgsbooks.com will be regularly reviewed and updated as needed.

Twenty-First Century Books
A division of Lerner Publishing Group, Inc.
241 First Avenue North
Minneapolis, MN 55401 U.S.A.

Website address: www.lernerbooks.com

web enhanced @ www.vgsbooks.com

Library of Congress Cataloging-in-Publication Data

Sirvaitis, Karen, 1961–
      Guyana in pictures / by Karen Sirvaitis.
         p.   cm. — (Visual geography series)
      Includes bibliographical references and index.
      ISBN: 978-1-57505-963-1 (lib. bdg. : alk. paper)
      1. Guyana—Juvenile literature. I. Title.
   F2368.5.S576 2010
   988.1—dc22   2009006295

                              4776

Manufactured in the United States of America
1 2 3 4 5 6 – BP – 15 14 13 12 11 10

INTRODUCTION

Guyana lies on the northeastern coast of South America. The nation is one of the poorest on the continent, yet it has an abundance of natural resources. These include the bounty of rain forests, gold, and untapped oil reserves.

Guyana is also one of the least populated countries in South America. This is partly because dense rain forests cover about 75 percent of the nation. Guyana's population of about 773,000 is a mix of ethnic backgrounds. People of African and East Indian ancestry dominate in numbers. Amerindians (native groups), Europeans, and Asians make up the minority. At times this ethnic mixture has led to tension and political strife.

Amerindian groups were the first people to live in Guyana. They probably arrived in the area about 3500 B.C. In the 1500s, Europeans began building colonies (settlements ruled by another country) in parts of South America. At first, the Europeans left present-day Guyana alone. They saw no signs of gold or other riches. And they thought

they would have a hard time surviving in Guyana's wilderness. But in the seventeenth century, Dutch settlers established a colony in Guyana and began to farm.

British planters followed the Dutch settlers. Eventually, Guyana became a colony of the British Empire. Both European groups relied on slave labor from Africa to run their plantations (large commercial farms). Most of Guyana's citizens of African descent trace their ancestry to these slaves.

In 1834 Great Britain abolished slavery in all its colonies. Therefore, planters shifted to the indenture (contract) system. Thousands of immigrants from India (East Indians) arrived in Guyana to work as indentured servants. The rich planters paid for the cost of getting the workers to Guyana. The planters also gave the indentured servants a place to live but paid low wages.

During the first half of the 1900s, the British still ruled Guyana. However, over time they gave working-class Guyanese more power.

By the 1950s, the Guyanese had created their first political parties. An Indo-Guyanese (Guyanese of East Indian descent) led one, and an Afro-Guyanese (Guyanese of African descent) led the other. The Guyanese believed that the ethnic group in power would benefit the most.

In 1966 Great Britain granted Guyana its independence. Violence between the nation's Indo-Guyanese and Afro-Guyanese marked the first elections. Conflict between the ethnic groups continued but usually only during elections.

In 1970 Guyana formed a Socialist government. Socialists believe in state control of the economy to ensure fair distribution of a nation's wealth. The government nationalized, or took over, most of Guyana's industries. By the late 1980s, however, Guyana was among the poorest nations in the region. To help the economy, Guyana's leaders changed the country's goals. In the 1990s, they sold some formerly government-owned industries to private owners.

In the twenty-first century, ethnic conflict based on politics is still an issue in Guyana. But in 2006, the nation held its first nonviolent election. In some ways, Guyana is more similar to its northern neighbors in the Caribbean Sea than it is to the countries of South America. Guyana and the Caribbean nations grow and export a lot of the same crops, including sugarcane and rice. In 2008 Guyana, along with other Caribbean nations, signed an Economic Partnership Agreement (EPA) with the European Union in hopes of increasing trade.

Meanwhile, Guyana is focusing on protecting its economy and the environment at the same time. The nation is coming up with creative ways to make money through preserving, rather than cutting down, its 40 million acres (16 million hectares) of rain forest. And Guyana must work to protect its heavily populated coast from flooding. Aging dams, dikes, and drainage canals need to be updated to confront seasonal flooding. Coastal communities also face a rising sea level due to global warming (changes in Earth's climate). Although the country faces challenges, it is determined to find solutions to its ongoing problems.

THE LAND

The Cooperative Republic of Guyana occupies 83,000 square miles (214,969 square kilometers) of territory on the northeastern coast of South America. The country is slightly smaller than the state of Minnesota. Guyana is bounded on the west by Venezuela, on the southwest by Brazil, and on the east by Suriname. Its northern boundary consists of 270 miles (435 km) of coastline on the Atlantic Ocean.

Amerindians first used the name "Guyana" (land of [many] waters) to refer to the triangle formed by the Orinoco, Amazon, and Negro rivers. The British used an English spelling of the name for their New World colony, British Guiana.

Topography

Guyana's landscape consists of three regions. Beginning at the Atlantic Ocean coast is a flat coastal strip. A belt of rolling hills and sandy soil follows. The third region is the interior highlands. These separate

landscape features are like three broad steps. Each one becomes higher and less accessible as the distance from the coast increases.

COASTAL PLAIN The coastal plain is a 10- to 40-mile-wide (16 to 64 km) strip of land along the Atlantic Ocean. Most of Guyana's population lives in the coastal plain, even though the region covers only 5 percent of Guyana's land. A majority of the country's agricultural production is in this area as well.

The coastal plain is made up of mudflats and beach ridges separated by low areas of marsh and swamp. Water helped to create the coastal plain. Over thousands of years, the rivers have carried sand, silt, and clay to the region. The forces of river and sea that created the fertile coastal plain also threaten human settlement there. The ocean washes away more soil than the rivers deposit. This causes much of the coastal land to erode (wear away) to below sea level.

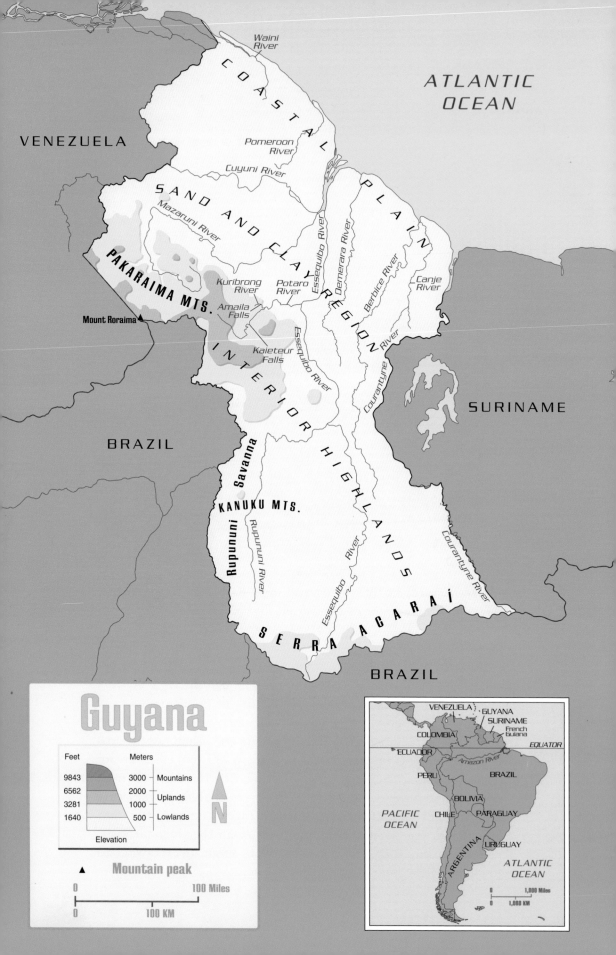

ATLANTIC OCEAN

VENEZUELA

Waini River

C O A S T A L

Pomeroon River

Cuyuni River

S A N D   A N D   C L A Y   P L A I N

Mazaruni River

PAKARAIMA MTS.

Kuribrong River

Potaro River

Essequibo River

Demerara River

Berbice River

Canje River

Mount Roraima ▲

Amaila Falls

Kaieteur Falls

Essequibo River

Courantyne River

R E G I O N

I N T E R I O R

SURINAME

BRAZIL

Savanna

KANUKU MTS.

H I G H L A N D S

Rupununi

Rupununi River

Essequibo River

Courantyne River

S E R R A   A C A R A Í

BRAZIL

Guyana

Feet	Meters	
9843	3000	Mountains
6562	2000	Uplands
3281	1000	Lowlands
1640	500	

Elevation

N

▲ **Mountain peak**

0   100 Miles

0   100 KM

VENEZUELA · GUYANA
SURINAME
French Guiana
COLOMBIA
EQUATOR
ECUADOR
Amazon River
PERU
BRAZIL
BOLIVIA
PACIFIC OCEAN
CHILE
PARAGUAY
ARGENTINA
URUGUAY
ATLANTIC OCEAN

1,000 Miles

1,000 KM

A **seawall** runs along the coast near the capital city of Georgetown to help prevent flooding. The sluice gate opens and closes to regulate the water level at different tides.

In some areas, farms and homes are as much as 10 feet (3 meters) below sea level. During heavy rains, the likelihood of flooding is strong. A system of dikes, dams, 140 miles (225 km) of ocean-facing seawall, and a network of drainage canals helps to make the land suitable for habitation. To adequately protect Guyana's coast from flooding, the system needs to be updated.

SAND AND CLAY REGION Inland from the coastal plain is a 150-mile-wide (241 km) belt of low, gently rolling terrain. The soil is a mixture of white sand and clay. Here and there, granite hills rise on the horizon. The coarse-grained sand comes from the erosion of these granite formations. The clay was formed by the deposit of fine silts during an earlier period when the ocean reached this far inland. This region supports much of the dense, tropical rain forest of Guyana.

INTERIOR HIGHLANDS The highest of the three regions is the interior highlands. It is made up of a series of flat-topped mountains and plateaus (flat areas). They range in elevation from 1,000 to 9,000 feet (305 to 2,743 m). The Pacaraima Mountains in the western interior form the largest range, both in area and in elevation. The range's highest peak—and the tallest point in the country—is Mount Roraima. It rises 9,094 feet (2,772 m). South and west of the Pakaraima range is a narrow area of savanna, or grassland. The tropical Rupununi Savanna sits near the Brazilian border. Its grasses provide pasture for

Guyana's small cattle industry. The Kanuku Mountains cut through the savanna. Farther south, also along the Brazilian border, is the Serra Acaraí, a low mountain range.

◉ Tides, Rivers, and Navigation

Spring ocean tides on Guyana's coast measure up to 8 feet (2 m) high. During high tide, seawater floods much of the unprotected coastal plain. A rising tide also creates the "tidal bore"—a surge of water that flows upstream, sometimes as far as 60 miles (97 km). During a tidal bore, it is impossible to paddle a canoe downstream against the strong incoming current. When the tide reverses, the streams carry not only their normal freshwater volume but additional salt water as well. With the greater volume of water, the current flows more quickly than usual.

Dozens of rivers crisscross Guyana. On a map, Guyana's rivers look like giant fallen trees. The main channels, which flow into the Atlantic Ocean, represent the trunks. The thousands of tributaries (branches) that drain the highlands form what look like tree branches. Most of the streams flow northward and eastward, from the interior mountains through the varied countryside. Spectacular waterfalls occur in the upper stream courses. Rapids endanger navigation on the lower reaches of the rivers.

Waterfalls and rapids of the interior highlands limit river navigation. They also provide the country with both hydroelectric (waterpower) potential and spectacular scenery. Beautiful Kaieteur Falls on the Potaro River—a western tributary of the Essequibo—has a sheer drop of 741 feet (226 m). This is nearly five times greater than Niagara Falls in North America.

Kaieteur Falls was named after Chief Kai of the Patamona tribe. According to legend, Chief Kai sacrificed his life on the falls to save his tribe. Visit www.vgsbooks.com for links to websites with additional information about Kaieteur Falls and the legend of Chief Kai.

Small boats and canoes are useful for traveling through shallow waters in Guyana's rivers.

The Essequibo is Guyana's largest river. It begins near the border with Brazil and flows 600 miles (966 km) toward the Atlantic Ocean. The Demerara River runs 230 miles (370 km) from eastern Guyana northward through the capital city of Georgetown before reaching the Atlantic. The Berbice River flows nearly 300 miles (483 km). It passes along the town of New Amsterdam before reaching the ocean. The 475-mile-long (764 km) Courantyne River forms Guyana's border with Suriname.

Large ships can navigate the major rivers only as far inland as the first rapids. But sandbars and mudflats pose a hazard for as much as 15 miles (24 km) inland from the coastline. Boats can travel on the Essequibo River for 40 miles (64 km) upstream from its mouth on the Atlantic Ocean. They can traverse the Courantyne and Demerara rivers for 60 miles (97 km). The Berbice River is navigable for 100 miles (161 km). Above the rapids of these rivers, navigation is limited to shallow boats and dugout canoes.

Climate

Guyana's temperatures reflect the climate of both the tropical rain forest and the tropical savanna. Heavy rainfall, high humidity, and hot temperatures are common. Greater differences in temperature occur between day and night than between seasons. Steady winds blow from the northeast during most of the year.

Average temperatures in Georgetown—about 80°F (27°C) year-round—are typical of the coastal region. The interior is far from the moderating influence of the sea. There, temperatures reach highs

of 103°F (39°C). Lows fall around 60°F (16°C) in the highlands.

Rainfall varies from an average of 80 inches (203 centimeters) a year in parts of the interior highlands to about 60 inches (152 cm) in the Rupununi region. Georgetown, on the coastal plain, however, receives an annual average of 90 inches (229 cm) of rain. These rainfall fluctuations are important to farmers. Their crops may fail due to drought (lack of rainfall) in some years and to excessive moisture at other times. Rain normally falls in short storms during the afternoon. Nearly half of the precipitation pours down during the rainy season from mid-April through mid-August. Another one-quarter falls during a shorter wet season from December through mid-February. The driest period in Guyana is from September through November. During this time, farmers gather the country's major crops—sugarcane and rice. Too much rain during harvest can cause serious flooding and crop losses.

Visit www.vgsbooks.com for links to websites with additional information about Guyana's land and climate. Learn more about the landscape of Guyana, and check out the weather conditions.

Flora and Fauna

Guyana can be divided into three major botanical regions—the coastal region, the interior forests, and the savannas. The weather, elevation, and soil in each region determine the kind of plant life it supports.

A mixture of trees and grasses grow along the coastal plain. To make room for homes and farms, people have cleared most of this natural vegetation. Even so, mangroves (trees that can live in salty water) and marsh grasses grow in the coastal swamps. These swamps merge gradually with inland freshwater marshes and heavily wooded swamps. As elevation increases and the land is drier, woodlands and savannas begin to appear.

About 75 percent of Guyana's territory consists of dense stands of tropical rain forest. The tropics is the region near Earth's equator, or central belt. Tropical areas are usually hot and humid, a climate in which many plants can thrive. Palm trees and giant kapok trees grow throughout the rain forest. Kapok trees reach upward to 200 feet (61 m) to compete for sunlight. Their broad trunks may measure over 20 feet (6 m) in diameter. Vines called lianas encircle the high branches. Many varieties of epiphytes—vegetation that grows on a host plant but takes its nourishment from the air and rain—are often visible. These epiphytes include numerous bromeliads (plants of the pineapple family) and orchids, as well as thousands of species of smaller plants. All the lush greenery presents an awesome collection of natural beauty.

In the southern interior, between the upper Essequibo River and the Brazilian border, the Rupununi Savanna has sparse grasses, occasional palm trees, and forests. Guyana's native grasses are low in nutrients, which cattle need to be healthy. Conditions have improved somewhat during recent years with the introduction of more nutritious grasses from other countries, particularly from Australia.

Guyana is a bird-watcher's paradise. In the forests, swarms of brilliant-hued macaws make their homes. Other parrots abound in the savanna. Ducks, snipes, plovers, herons, and many other shorebirds live along the coast. Inland streams host ibis and kingfishers. These wading birds use their long bills to fish the shallow waters. Vampire bats, found throughout Central and South America, live off the blood of large birds and animals. Guyana works to control its population of vampire bats because they are notorious for spreading rabies, a deadly disease.

Guyana's rivers are home to a variety of fish. The giant arapaima is a freshwater fish that grows up to 7 feet (2 m) long. Piranhas (small fish with teeth) travel in groups in rivers and streams. Though they eat land mammals such as small deer that wander into rivers, their presence does not prevent the Guyanese from swimming.

Reptiles, including the flesh-eating black caiman (a small crocodile), also live in Guyana's rivers. Many varieties of lizards and poisonous snakes slither throughout Guyana's rain forests. The most common venomous snakes are the himeralli (a coral snake), the labarria, and the bushmaster.

UNMATCHED ABUNDANCE

Tropical rain forests have a greater number and variety of plants and animals than any other location on Earth. The list of different species is long. At least 1,500 species of flowering plants, 750 species of trees, 125 species of mammals, 400 species of birds, 100 species of reptiles, 60 species of amphibians, and 150 species of butterflies can be found within just a 4-square-mile (10 sq. km) section of rain forest. Researchers are just beginning to learn about some of the plants. More than 2,000 different tropical rain forest plants, for instance, may have properties that can prevent or even treat cancer. Scientists are researching how to make medicines out of these plants.

A great variety of mammals inhabit Guyana's land—and water. Antillean manatees, or sea cows, live in Guyana's shallow coastal waters and sometimes in rivers. These large and gentle creatures are the world's only aquatic herbivore— or mammal that lives in the water and eats plants. Among the largest native mammals in South America, they grow to 12 feet (4 m) long and weigh as much as 1,500 pounds (680 kilograms). People have overhunted manatees for their flesh, and they are endangered, or threatened with dying out completely.

Another animal that has been hunted almost to the point of extinction is the tapir. Tapirs are the largest and strangest-looking land animals in Guyana. They are about the size of a pony, but they can grow up to 700 pounds (318 kg). Their stubby trunks make them look like a mix between a pig and an elephant. They are related to the horse and rhinoceros.

The Botanical Gardens in Georgetown keeps about a dozen **manatees** in its canals. The park sometimes loans the animals to towns with irrigation canals. The manatees, who love plants, keep the canals clean by eating unwanted vegetation.

Giant anteaters tear at the concrete-hard surfaces of tall anthills with their 4-inch (10 cm) claws, in search of food. Jaguars prowl through the forest, while spider and howler monkeys travel noisily through the canopy of trees. The capybara is a piglike rodent that grows up to 4 feet (1 m) long and weighs as much as 100 pounds (45 kg). Peccaries are small wild pigs that travel in groups of about one hundred. People hunt capybaras, peccaries, and several varieties of deer for food.

Natural Resources and the Environment

Guyana's rain forests provide the nation with numerous natural resources, namely timber, medicinal plants, rare wildlife, and fish. The trees in Guyana's rain forests offer a rich supply of timber. But clearing, or cutting down, rain forest trees has serious consequences for the entire planet. Half the world's plant and animal species reside in rain forests. Without rain forests, these species (including plants that can be used as medicine) could disappear. When Guyana cuts down trees for timber, it contributes to global warming. Global warming is an unnatural warming of Earth's atmosphere.

Guyana has made protecting its rain forests a priority. The government established Iwokrama International Centre for Rain Forest Conservation and Development. Iwokrama is a 1-million-acre (371,000-hectare) rain forest preserve in the heart of Guyana. Workers here study tropical forest management.

Some approaches to managing Guyana's forests include limiting the number of trees that can be cut down each year. Land managers have placed fishing limits on the arapaima, the mammoth fish whose numbers have recently suffered. Cracking down on poachers and banning the capture and export of rare birds and butterflies help to protect biodiversity (the abundance and variety of wildlife).

In addition to the rain forest, Guyana harvests seafood in the Atlantic Ocean. Shrimp is a common catch. To ensure an ongoing

GLOBAL WARMING

Tropical deforestation (loss of trees) is a leading cause of global warming, or the warming of Earth's atmosphere. Global warming is caused by a buildup of gases, such as carbon dioxide, in the upper layers of the atmosphere. Trees are about 50 percent carbon. When felled, they release their stored carbon into the atmosphere. When left standing, trees and other plants absorb carbon dioxide. Fewer trees mean more carbon dioxide gets in the atmosphere. Deforestation contributes at least 20 percent of the world's total gas emissions.

FOSSIL FUEL

People usually burn fossil fuels (such as oil and coal) to generate heat and electricity and to power cars. When burned, fossil fuels release carbon dioxide into Earth's atmosphere.

Researchers measure a nation's carbon emissions by determining the amount of carbon dioxide released into the atmosphere when people burn fossil fuels. In 2004 Guyana's carbon dioxide emissions per capita were 2.3 tons (2 metric tons), which is low compared to more developed countries. Many rural areas of Guyana lack electricity, and most Guyanese do not own a car.

supply of seafood, Guyanese fishing crews must be careful not to over-fish the waters offshore.

Most of the country's mineral wealth is in the sand and clay region. Miners delve widely to reach deposits of bauxite (the main ingredient in aluminum) and gold. Diamonds and manganese also exist in the region, as well as smaller quantities of other ores.

Mining involves a number of environmental risks. To get at the minerals, miners cut down trees and dig wide, deep pits in the ground. Some mining companies remove the minerals from the pits with the aid of harmful chemicals. They allow sediment to pollute nearby streams and rivers. Once miners have stripped out the gold or bauxite, the pit is abandoned. Trees can no longer grow in these pits, which are void of topsoil. The harsh effects of mining are a source of trouble mainly for Guyana's Amerindians, who live in scattered communities throughout the region's rain forests. The Amerindians fish and drink water from the polluted streams that flow from the sand and clay region into the rain forests.

Cities

Guyana has three major cities—Georgetown, New Amsterdam, and Linden. Unemployment is a concern in Guyana's cities. Many educated city dwellers leave Guyana to find employment in other countries. Laborers sometimes go inland to log the rain forests or to work in the mines. These workers stay in camps for months at a time.

GEORGETOWN is Guyana's capital and largest city, with a population of close to 150,000. The British named the city after George III, an eighteenth-century British king. Georgetown lies along Guyana's central coast, near the mouth of the Demerara River. It is Guyana's chief port. The capital's wide streets form a grid pattern. Canals run through the middle of some of the broader boulevards. The business district lies along the river, while the government offices are grouped in the center of town. Most houses and other buildings are wooden. They often perch on brick piers or stilts to raise them above the damp coastal ground.

No other cities or towns in Guyana rival the importance of Georgetown. Smaller settlements, such as New Amsterdam and Linden, provide other regions with their own focal point.

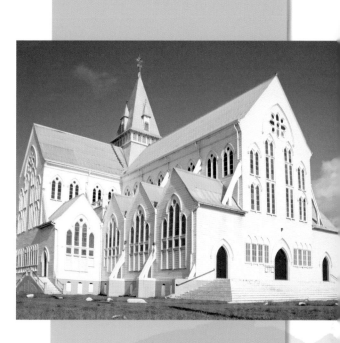

NEW AMSTERDAM (population 18,000) is an old Dutch town in northeastern Guyana on the east bank of the Berbice River. Like in Georgetown, about 55 miles (89 km) away, New Amsterdam's homes rest on stilts and sit aboveground to guard against flooding. As a port city, New Amsterdam ships sugar, rice, cattle products, and lumber.

LINDEN (population 29,000) is a newer settlement, linked to the capital city by a good road. The town lies 70 miles (113 km) up the Demerara River and is involved in bauxite mining.

SAINT GEORGE'S CATHEDRAL

Reaching 145 feet (44 m) high, Saint George's Cathedral in Georgetown is the tallest wooden structure in South America—and one of the tallest in the world. The cathedral was built in 1892. All the wood is from local trees, except the ceilings. British architect Arthur Blomfield designed the church to have a light and airy feel. An ornate wooden screen separates the altar from the seating area. A large pipe organ contributes to the church's elaborate interior.

HISTORY AND GOVERNMENT

As early as 3500 B.C., many Amerindian groups may have already inhabited Guyana. The Warao, a peaceful group whose name means "canoe people," lived in the area near the mouth of the Orinoco in present-day Venezuela. They eventually spread into western Guyana. The Arawak, a friendly, peace-loving tribe, lived between the Courantyne and Waini rivers. The largest group was the Caribs. They probably arrived sometime in the fourteenth century. They came from the south, by crossing through modern-day Brazil. At first they lived in Guyana's heavily forested interior. Eventually, they went farther north, reaching the Caribbean islands.

Most of Guyana's Amerindians did not settle in permanent villages but moved from place to place. For food, they hunted animals with bows and arrows and fished with hooks, nets, and a poisoned piece of bark used as a spear. About two to three thousand years ago, some groups started to plant crops of cassava (a root vegetable), corn, yams, cotton, and tobacco. When the crops depleted the farmland

of its nutrients, the Amerindians cleared more land or moved. They slept in comfortable and portable hammocks they made from cotton and twine. They lived in round huts made of wood and cane with thatched roofs.

Although the different Amerindian groups shared some customs, their lifestyles varied in many ways. The Caribs were fiercely independent warriors and seafarers. They were expert swimmers who built huge dugout canoes out of tree trunks. These canoes could withstand the strong currents of Guyana's rivers and the sea. They settled in villages but relied more on hunting than on farming. Their government consisted of chieftains and an *ouboutou*, or an elected military leader. An ouboutou would organize raids against other Amerindian groups, stealing food, possessions, and people.

The Arawak were a peaceful and gentle people who sometimes needed to escape from the less friendly Caribs. Arawak families lived together in villages. Sometimes groups of villages banded together for protection from Carib raids. A cacique, or chieftain, led the villagers, who freely shared all food and property. The Arawak practiced a religion called Zemism. They worshipped their ancestors and many nature gods and goddesses, called zemis.

The Arawak language does not have a word for "war."

The Warao lived in an isolated, marshy area near many rivers. They relied on dugout canoes for transportation. Water surrounded the Warao, and the children learned to paddle a canoe before they learned to walk. The Warao preferred to gather, rather than grow, most of their food. They ate crabs and other shellfish. And they depended on the ita palm, called "the tree of life." Ita palm trees provided the Warao with a fruit rich in vitamin A and with a drinkable sap. The Warao lived in huts without walls. The huts were built on stilts to protect the buildings from wet ground. Because of the Warao's location, they did not need to worry much about Carib attacks.

Early European Exploration

Christopher Columbus is the first European known to have seen the coast of Guyana. In 1498, during his third voyage to the New World, Columbus only viewed the low-lying tropical coast of present-day Guyana from his sailing vessel. A year later, Spanish explorer Alonso de Ojeda became the first European to set foot on the land. The Spaniards did not try to settle in the area, which was inhabited

Alonso de Ojeda and the Spanish explorers meet with Amerindians in around 1500.

by Caribs. They were familiar with the warlike Caribs, who fiercely resisted European contact.

In addition, the Spaniards did not consider the area to be of any use. They could not find any mineral wealth in the region. The coastal mangrove swamps and the many marshlands made the territory appear useless for agriculture or settlement. Moreover, navigation was hazardous due to vast coastal mudflats and frequent sandbars in the rivers. The Spaniards left Guyana. European explorers would not return to the area for another one hundred years.

El Dorado ("the Golden One" in Spanish) was a mythical land based on a legend about an Indian leader who covered his body with gold dust each morning and washed it off in a lake each evening. Some European explorers believed El Dorado was a real place in northern South America. They also believed that whoever found it would be extremely rich.

In 1593 the search for El Dorado began in the Guyana region. During that year, Pedro da Silva led an ill-fated Spanish expedition. They searched the Orinoco region in vain for the hidden golden land. Fewer than fifty people survived the ordeal.

Walter Raleigh

Between 1595 and 1616, Walter Raleigh of England led three expeditions to the Guyana territory in search of El Dorado. Although Raleigh failed to locate any gold, he made friendly contact with the region's Arawak. Raleigh described the area's natural attractions in his book *Discoverie of the Large, Riche and Bewtiful Empyre of Guiana*. The ship's mapmaker drew the first accurate portrayal of Guyana's coastline.

Dutch Colonization

The Dutch were the first Europeans to gain a real foothold in Guyana. They were interested in making money. They wanted to find good farmland to raise crops that could only grow in hot climates. They could export the crops to Europe for a profit. The location, however, had to be easily defended against attacks by Spaniards. The Spanish had settled other parts of South America and the Caribbean.

In 1616 Dutch colonists selected a site on an island bluff. It overlooked the junction of the Mazaruni and Cuyuni rivers, about 40 miles (64 km) upstream from the mouth of the Essequibo.

The settlement was named Kyk-Over-al (Overlooking All). The settlers tried growing coffee, tobacco, and cotton. But without a large workforce, they could only clear and plow small tracts of land. If the settlers were going to make money, they were going to need to plant a lot more crops.

Meanwhile in Europe, the Dutch government granted a charter, or legal right, to the Dutch West India Company. The charter, issued in 1621, gave the company complete political and economic control over the territory it called Guiana. The company could conduct pirate raids against Spanish shipping and transport slaves from western Africa to the New World, including to Guiana.

With a slave labor force of men and women stolen from their homes in Africa, the farms began to grow in size and in yield. The success of the Dutch venture encouraged the development of other plantations. Similar settlements appeared along the Berbice, the Demerara, and the Pomeroon rivers. The Berbice district became a separate territory in 1732, and a Demerara district was established in 1741. These two districts were not governed by the Dutch West India Company but by other Dutch officials.

Guyana's inland plantations were not fertile enough to grow much cotton and tobacco. Guyana, therefore, could not compete with the output of these crops from other South American colonies. With the presence of the Dutch West India Company, the threat of Spanish attack had diminished. Dutch colonists felt safe to move to Guyana's fertile coast.

Developing New Farmland

On the coast, the Dutch planned to grow sugarcane. Sugarcane, used to make sugar and rum, was a valuable crop. Sugar was becoming a popular sweetener in Europe. But to plant crops along the coast, the Dutch had to improve the coastal plains' low-lying and poorly drained land. This required something the Dutch were already famous for—poldering, or creating tracts of land protected from water on all sides. To create polders, workers construct an elaborate network of dikes, floodgates, and irrigation and drainage canals. Only wealthy colonists could afford such undertakings. They built only a few large plantations. These wealthy plantation owners held a monopoly on sugar and tobacco production within the colony.

To create Guyana's coastal polders, African slaves moved an estimated 100 million tons (91 million metric tons) of mud by hand.

During this period of rapid expansion, a Dutchman named Laurens Storm van's Gravesande provided energetic leadership. He was the director-general of the Essequibo and Demerara districts. He encouraged the further opening up of the Demerara lands and the movement of planters to the shores of the Essequibo. Here, settlers found rich farmland and precious minerals, including gold and diamonds. Gravesande's contributions over a period of thirty years established him as the most important figure in the early colonial history of Guyana.

Beginning in the mid-eighteenth century, British planters from the West Indies were attracted to the fertile lands of the Demerara region as well. These new settlers expanded their plantations inland, rather

A Dutch slave master claims ownership of people who have just arrived in Guyana on a slave ship in 1806.

than along the coast. Thus, sugar plantations evolved as long, narrow strips of land reaching from the coast toward the interior. By 1760 the British made up more than half of Demerara's European population.

By 1780 the number of British settlers throughout Guyana was so great that the Dutch colony was effectively under British influence. In 1781 war broke out between the Dutch and the British over ownership of the colony. The war resulted in the British winning control over Guyana. A year later, the French seized power and governed for two years. During their rule, they created the town of Longchamps at the mouth of the Demerara River. When the Dutch regained power in 1784, they moved their colonial capital to Longchamps and renamed it Stabroek.

CUFFY

The cruel conditions settlers imposed on the black labor force caused frequent rebellions. In 1763 a house slave named Cuffy headed the most famous revolt. He led a group of slaves from the Magdalenenburg Plantation on the banks of the Canje River in the Berbice district. Cuffy's immediate plan was to obtain more humane treatment for slaves. His long-range goal was to free fifteen thousand slaves. For nearly a year, the Africans controlled Berbice. But eventually Berbice governor Wolfert Simon van Hoogenheim suppressed the revolt. The rebels had killed more than four thousand plantation owners and overseers. Cuffy is revered in Guyana's history as a national hero for his early role in the cause of freedom.

People of Guyana erected a **monument to Cuffy** in Georgetown.

British Rule

The Dutch maintained control over the Essequibo, Demerara, and Berbice settlements until 1796. That year a British fleet from the Caribbean island of Barbados conquered the country. The British governed until 1802. Then, under a truce established by the Treaty of Amiens, the Dutch again claimed Guyana.

In 1803 the British once again conquered the colony. In 1814, under agreements contained in the Treaty of Paris and the Congress of Vienna, European discord over the Guianas finally ended. The French secured French Guiana. The Dutch took over the territory of present-day Suriname, which was then called Dutch Guiana. And the British paid the Dutch the equivalent of $15 million for Britain's slice of the Guiana region, which it called British Guiana.

Under British rule, trade and population increased rapidly. The plantations were at their peak, and the slave population numbered more than one hundred thousand people. During this time, the British renamed Stabroek Georgetown, after the British king George III. They also made it more modern. They built schools and libraries. The British continued the Dutch project of reclaiming land from the sea. And they began to increase transportation by constructing roads, bridges, canals, and a railway.

Abolition of Slavery

In 1807 the British government started the process of ending the slave trade throughout its empire. Planters could keep the slaves they owned at the time but could not buy new ones. To ensure an ongoing supply of labor, plantation owners required their slaves to have children.

The British Parliament formally abolished (outlawed) slavery on August 1, 1834, throughout all British colonies. To help ease the transition, the British required former slaves to work for their former owners for four years. During this time, planters paid the freed slaves wages and housed and clothed them in exchange for their services. In August 1838, the former slaves were free to go. The government paid planters 50 British pounds (about $250) for each slave they were forced to release.

For many years, sugar was a luxury item in Great Britain, consumed only by the wealthy. By the 1800s, common people had begun to enjoy it as well. At this time, Britain's consumption of sugar increased by 2,500 percent. Guyana's plantation owners made a lot of money exporting the sweetener to Great Britain.

◉ The Indenture System

Faced with a shortage of workers, planters searched for another system that would provide low-wage labor. The landowners decided to import workers under a system of indentured servitude. This arrangement meant that in return for free passage to British Guiana, a person signed a contract to work for a fixed number of years. Landowners provided workers with basic needs, such as food, water, and shelter, as well as a meager wage.

> After the ending of slavery, few former slaves chose to work—even for wages—for the plantation owners who had once enslaved them. Farm production declined drastically, falling by 60 percent between 1839 and 1842. Ten years after the abolition of slavery, the number of plantations had dropped from 230 to 180. Only 16 of the 174 coffee and cotton plantations were still in operation.

Immigrants under this system included people from Portugal, China, the West Indies, and Africa. But there were still not enough laborers. A wealthy plantation owner named John Gladstone proposed that Guyana bring in workers from India to work on the plantations. The first East Indian immigrants arrived in 1838. Within about five years, they began arriving in droves.

The East Indians were subject to a five-year indenture period. After five years, they were free to return to India at their own expense. After a ten-year period of service, the government paid for passage back to their homeland.

Robert Hermann Schomburgk

◉ Border Disputes

In the mid-nineteenth century, Britain had sent German explorer Robert Hermann Schomburgk to define the borders of its Guiana colony. His boundaries included territories that Brazil and Venezuela had traditionally called their own. In 1880 gold was discovered within the area claimed by both British Guiana and Venezuela. A dispute arose over ownership of the land.

Britain was a strong imperial power, and Venezuela was comparatively weak. Great Britain eventually agreed to sub-

mit its claim to an international commission. The commission—made up of two Venezuelans, two British, and one Russian—moved the boundaries slightly. But they awarded ownership of the disputed area largely to British Guiana.

Colonial Imbalance of Power

Since the arrival of the Dutch, rich European planters had held most of the political power. Toward the end of the nineteenth century, only a small percentage—mainly wealthy male plantation owners—could vote. Neither former slaves nor indentured workers could claim any political influence.

This political imbalance became intolerable to Afro-Guyanese (Guyanese of African descent) and Indo-Guyanese (Guyanese of East Indian descent). Together the two groups formed the bulk of the population, yet they had no political power. In 1891 the working class of British Guiana sent a petition to Britain's queen, Victoria. In it, they asked for representation in the British government. In response, Britain added several elected, rather than appointed, officials to the Combined Court. The Combined Court was a small group of plantation owners. Guyana's governor appointed them to handle legislative, administrative, and financial matters. Adding elected officials slightly reduced the control of the wealthy. But British Guiana was still a long way from democracy.

At the height of the British Empire under Queen Victoria (reigned 1837–1901), Britain governed territory covering about one-quarter of the world.

The majority of Guyanese continued to be discontent about a lack of political power into the twentieth century. In November 1905, a group of stevedores, or dock laborers, decided to strike. They refused to do any work unless they received higher wages. Other workers joined the stevedores. On December 1, 1905—a day remembered as Black Friday—colonial authorities opened fire on the protesters at Plantation Ruimveldt, just outside of Georgetown. Word of the shootings spread, and before long, rioting broke out throughout Georgetown. By the end of the day, seven people had been killed and more than a dozen injured.

Not long after these clashes, Britain called on its colonies—including British Guiana—to help the empire fight in World War I (1914–1918). Most of the battles of World War I took place in Europe and the Middle East. But the war affected Guyana and other European colonies worldwide. Colonial powers, including Britain and Germany, called on their colonies to provide soldiers. Afro-Guyanese who fought for the British overseas came back to Guyana with an increased status. The war also promoted the cause of Guyana's Indo-Guyanese, who were still bonded by the indenture system. India, also a British colony, had willingly sent more than a million troops to help the British army. Indian nationalists (people who wanted India to be independent of British rule) argued for the end of indentured servitude. In 1917 British Guiana ended the indenture system. This method of obtaining cheap labor had satisfied the planter's demand for workers for nearly eighty years, but it was not fair to the workers.

Changes in Power

After the war, in the 1920s, trade unions established a strong foothold in the colony. Groups of workers from different industries united under the British Guiana Labour Union (BGLU). Their goal was to get companies to pay them fair wages and to ensure safe working conditions. If their demands weren't met, they threatened to go on strike. Without a workforce, companies would lose customers and money. Trade unionism had become a powerful force in Britain as well. In 1928 the British government ordered all of its colonies to work with unions.

In the same year, a one-house Legislative Council replaced the planter-dominated Combined Court. This move took some power away from sugarcane plantation owners but put it in the hands of rice producers and mining companies. Most of the council's members were appointed, and only a small minority of colonists qualified as voters. Britain settled most policy decisions, and a crown-appointed governor carried out the orders. Most Guyanese had less political power than before.

War once again broke out in Europe, when Germany invaded Poland in 1939. During World War II (1939–1945), Britain again focused on warfare. For Guyana these years became a time of change. Guyana governor

Sir Gordon Lethem stands on a balcony in Georgetown to announce Germany's surrender during World War II on May 8, 1945.

Sir Gordon Lethem encouraged reforms. Lethem legalized political parties, allowed more citizens to vote—including women—and increased the number of elected officials on the Legislative Council.

The Road to Independence

Guyana's road to independence was a rocky one. In 1950 Cheddi Jagan (an Indo-Guyanese) and Forbes Burnham (an Afro-Guyanese) created a political party called the People's Progressive Party (PPP). In 1953 a new constitution granted all adult citizens the right to vote and established a two-house legislature. But political turmoil followed the first general election. The British government feared that the PPP promoted Communism. Communism is a form of government that aims to create a classless society, where all people are equal. It also promotes changing the way an economy operates by placing all businesses under government ownership. In addition to the PPP's suspected political leanings, the party also pushed for independence from Britain. Consequently, the British suspended the new constitution and the elected government.

From 1954 until new elections were held in 1957, an interim government ruled British Guiana. Meanwhile, Jagan and Burnham had a disagreement. Burnham left the PPP in 1955. Two years later, he formed the People's National Congress (PNC), which eventually became an opposition party to the PPP. From this time forward, ethnic background divided the majority of Guyana's citizens. Most Afro-Guyanese supported Burnham and the PNC. Most Indo-Guyanese supported Jagan and the PPP.

Cheddi Jagan celebrates his election victory in 1961.

The new constitution finally went into effect in 1961. Voters elected Jagan prime minister later that year. The Afro-Guyanese feared Indo-Guyanese domination, which sparked widespread riots in Georgetown. British troops arrived, and a general strike broke out. Months of chaos followed. In a heavily contested election in 1964 between Jagan and Burnham, the colonial governor declared Burnham the victor.

Independence

Throughout these unsettled years, British Guiana was still a colony. In 1966 Britain granted Guyana its independence. Forbes Burnham became prime minister of the new nation, renamed Guyana. But corruption followed the elation of achieving independence. The PPP accused Burnham's government of rigging, or controlling the outcome of, elections. Burnham lost much of his support.

In 1970, under Burnham's leadership, Guyana became a Socialist nation, in which the government played a large role in managing the economy. It also controlled social services such as health care. The Guyanese government nationalized, or took over, foreign-owned companies that produced much of the country's wealth. Burnham virtually ended international trade by refusing to allow imports into the country. This created shortages of basic goods such as flour and many manufactured items. Under Burnham, educated Guyanese began leaving the country in record numbers, seeking jobs and a higher quality of life elsewhere.

Jim Jones's family posed for this portrait in 1976. Jim and his wife are seated *(center)*.

Burnham ruled Guyana for nineteen years until his death in August 1985. By then the government controlled more than three-quarters of the country's economy. In addition, a new constitution made the president the head of the country. Immediately following Burnham's death, Vice President Hugh Desmond Hoyte was sworn into office. In December Guyana held its regularly scheduled elections. Many observers criticized the election process. They accused Hoyte and his party of claiming votes from people who either didn't exist or were not eligible to vote. Hoyte and the PNC won a solid victory. Many people regarded this as a sign that little in Guyanese politics had changed.

The Guyanese government carried out important electoral reforms in the early 1990s. New voter lists replaced former, fraudulent lists.

JONESTOWN TRAGEDY

The People's Temple was a California-based religious cult led by the Reverend Jim Jones. In the 1970s, the Guyanese government gave Jones permission to build a religious center called Jonestown in Guyana's western region, near Port Kaituma. The enterprise ended in tragedy, however. The U.S. government began investigating Jones and his methods for keeping members of his church. In response, on November 18, 1978, the paranoid leader ordered the nine hundred–plus members of Jonestown to commit mass suicide by drinking cyanide-laced grape-flavored juice. Many who tried to escape were shot and killed. Only a handful of people survived to tell the story.

Left: **Cheddi Jagan** speaks at a 1993 news conference at the White House.
Right: Janet Jagan became the **first woman president** of Guyana in 1997.

Voting in October 1992 brought the PPP to power. Cheddi Jagan became president.

Cheddi Jagan returned 80 percent of businesses to private ownership. He also worked to improve Guyanese education, housing, and sanitation. He remained in office until his death in 1997. Later that same year, voters elected his wife, Janet Jagan, to be Guyana's first woman president. She resigned from office in 1999 due to poor health. Finance minister Bharrat Jagdeo, who had been named prime minister the day before Jagan resigned, immediately succeeded her as president.

The Twenty-first Century

In 2001 Bharrat Jagdeo ran for president and won, but not without strife. Rioting followed, as those aligned with the PNC claimed election fraud. Jagdeo triumphed again in 2006, in an election that foreign observers considered fair. That year Guyana held its first nonviolent election in twenty years.

Jagdeo has actively pursued opportunities to improve Guyana's struggling

President Jagdeo

economy. He has successfully bargained for debt relief (when international lenders cancel or minimize the amount of money owed to them). One condition of debt relief is that Guyana must use the money it saves to reduce poverty in the country. Jagdeo also focuses on finding new ways for Guyana to bring more dollars into the impoverished country. Jagdeo has offered to lease, or rent, portions of the rain forest to foreign companies. These foreign leasers benefit by earning money from rain forest tourism, from medicines made from rare tropical plants, and from accruing carbon credits (unused allowances of carbon dioxide gas emissions). Because of their understanding of the plants and animals in the rain forest, Amerindians have become an important part of the plans to preserve the rain forests. Their input is crucial to establishing laws and guidelines for managing a sustainable forest.

In 2007 the United Nations (an international organization that promotes worldwide peace and security) helped Guyana and Suriname settle a dispute over boundaries within the sea. The maritime boundary disagreement arose several years earlier, when Guyana granted a Canadian company the right to drill for oil about 100 miles (160 km) off Guyana's coast. Suriname brought military gunboats to the site. They ordered that the oil rig stop, claiming that the Canadians were within Surinamese waters. The United Nations Law of the Sea tribunal

CARBON CREDIT

When a company buys a stake in preserving Guyana's rain forest, it can also buy rights to the carbon stored in the forest's timber. Why would it want the carbon? Technically, it doesn't want the carbon itself. It wants credit for not cutting down the trees, which release carbon dioxide into the atmosphere. Carbon dioxide is a greenhouse gas that contributes to global warming. The global community is requiring companies worldwide to limit the amount of carbon dioxide they create. If a company produces more carbon dioxide than is permitted, the company has to pay a fee. If a company produces less carbon dioxide than is permitted, the company can sell its extra carbon—its carbon credits—to companies that produce too much carbon. The overpolluting companies can avoid heavy fines by buying the carbon credits.

Critics of this system argue that selling carbon credits permits the polluting companies to avoid changing their ways. Others say that it encourages companies to pollute less so they can sell their extra carbon credits.

Members of Guyana's assembly meet inside this **parliament building** in Georgetown. African slaves built the structure in the 1800s.

determined that most of the area belonged to Guyana. Guyana's boundary dispute with Venezuela has not yet been resolved. Venezuela claims about two-thirds of Guyana, from the Essequibo River west.

In the twenty-first century, Guyana is helping to ease the political tensions between its two largest ethnic groups—the Indo-Guyanese and the Afro-Guyanese—by working to stop election fraud. Guyana also seeks to balance worldwide environmental concerns with the right to use its natural resources (the rain forest) to generate income. And to reverse the steady flow of people leaving the nation, Guyana is trying to improve the overall quality of life for its citizens.

Visit www.vgsbooks.com for links to websites with additional information about political developments in Guyana. Read local news headlines, and follow Guyana's efforts to ease political tensions between the country's ethnic groups.

Government

Guyana's first constitution became effective on May 26, 1966, which is celebrated as Guyanese Independence Day. In February 1970, Guyana declared itself a sovereign democratic republic, ending its ties with British rule.

In accordance with the 1980 constitution, a president heads the government. A separate, one-house national assembly (group of lawmakers) of sixty-five members is elected to five-year terms. The president is the leader of the majority party in the legislature. The presidential term lasts for the duration of the assembly. The president appoints the prime minister, who serves as head of government and is a member of the cabinet, or a group of advisers.

Although the constitution is the supreme law of the land, Guyana also has two legal traditions—British common law and the Dutch code. Magistrate courts handle small monetary claims, and a higher court has jurisdiction in civil and criminal matters.

Guyana is divided into ten regions. A chairperson heads each region. Villages and towns have city councils to vote on local issues. Amerindian Village Councils have their own legislation.

> Heavy rains in January 2005 caused serious flooding along Guyana's populated coast. The system of dams, dikes, and drainage canals needs updating to prepare for the possibility of more flooding.

THE PEOPLE

"One people, one nation, one destiny" reads the motto on Guyana's coat of arms. Yet, unlike the people in most South American countries, Guyanese have remained largely separated by their ethnic background. The population numbers about 773,000. Of the thirteen South American countries, Guyana ranks eleventh in population. Part of the reason for the low population is because 75 percent of the country is covered by dense rain forest. Only Suriname and French Guiana have fewer people.

Most Guyanese live in the coastal plain along the Atlantic Ocean. This region occupies less than 5 percent of the country, yet it supports almost 90 percent of the population. Here people farm, work in factories, or in the capital city of Georgetown. Guyanese who live and work in the interior are usually involved in mining, raising livestock, logging, or tourism. Because most of the interior region is difficult to reach by road, mining and logging companies set up temporary camps for employees. Small, isolated communities are found in the interior rain forests.

Ethnic Groups

Guyana's largest ethnic groups are people of East Indian (49 percent) or of African (36 percent) ancestry. Approximately 7 percent of the population is of mixed race. Another 7 percent are Amerindian. (The name Amerindians is used for Guyana's native groups to distinguish them from the immigrant East Indian population.) The remaining 1 percent are from other backgrounds. Chinese, Portuguese, British, and Amerindian peoples all have contributed to the cultural heritage of the nation.

In Guyana the dominant people culturally are the Afro-Guyanese. They are descended mainly from slaves brought from western Africa in the seventeenth, eighteenth, and nineteenth centuries. Survivors of a transplanted African heritage, these Guyanese have largely adopted European culture. Some Afro-Guyanese live in small villages and farming communities, but most dwell in towns or in the capital city.

Most Indo-Guyanese claim the Ganges Valley of northern India and various parts of southern India as the source of their cultural roots. The first arrivals came over as indentured laborers. Most of their descendants live in rural areas along the coast.

More than thirty thousand Amerindians live in Guyana. They are descendants of the earliest inhabitants of northeastern South America. Amerindians are the most isolated group of Guyanese. Most of them live in scattered communities throughout the rain forest. Other Amerindians inhabit the more remote coastal regions. Many Amerindians are knowledgeable about the plant and animal life in the rain forest, where as a people they have hunted and fished for centuries. These groups still live off the land and practice many of their ancient traditions. They use the farming methods their ancestors developed. Other Amerindians, however, have partly accepted European ways. They wear Western clothing and speak English. They may take jobs in Georgetown or work on cattle ranches or in the mines.

Three generations of Amerindians from the Arawak tribe

Two **Indo-Guyanese** people sit at a cafe in Georgetown. Almost half of Guyana's population is of East Indian descent.

Language

Guyana was the only British colony in South America. It is the only country in South America where English is the official language. Most Afro-Guyanese speak a form of English called Creole. Creole is a blend of European and African dialects. Some Indo-Guyanese speak Hindi, Tamil, or Telugu—all major Indian languages. Only about 2 percent of Indo-Guyanese can write these languages. Each of a dozen native groups speaks a different ancient dialect. Not much is known about the history of the Warao language. It is very different from any other known Amerindian language in South America and the Caribbean.

Languages, like animals, can become endangered. Guyanese educators are working with Amerindian groups to ensure that their languages are passed on to

PROVERB

Proverbs, or short sayings that communicate important beliefs, are popular in Guyana. Following are several common Guyanese proverbs, written with a Creole accent.

- "Wuh fall from head drop pun shoulder." (Sins of the parents fall on the children.)
- "Mocking is ketching." (Don't laugh at another's situation, it might be yours.)
- "Mouth open, story jump out." (Some people can't keep a secret.)
- "Show me yuh company, I'll tell you who you be." (People judge you by the friends you keep.)

—*Gale Encyclopedia of Multicultural America*, 2000

new generations. Amerindians who move to the cities and adopt the English language and European ways sometimes do not teach their children their native language and customs. Because so few Amerindians remain in the country, preserving these ancient languages has become a national priority.

Rural and Urban Lifestyles

Guyana has the highest proportion of rural population in South America. About 62 percent of Guyanese live in the countryside. Many Guyanese are farmers who grow sugarcane and rice on the same plantations the Dutch and British first started. Miners and loggers also lead rural lifestyles. Many of them leave their homes for months at a time to work in the country's scantly populated interior. Loggers fell trees in the rain forest. Miners work in the pits, some of which are also deep within the rain forest.

Guyana's cities have been declining in population. Nearly 83 percent of Guyanese who graduate from college leave Guyana to seek better opportunities. Most city dwellers work in factories, processing sugar or minerals. But these opportunities are limited.

A path winds through a rural Amerindian settlement.

Guyanese residents spend time on bustling **Regent Street,** one of the busiest streets in Georgetown.

Guyana is among the poorest nations of South America. One-third of Guyana's population lives below the poverty level. Many people are without electricity and plumbing. Most homes are wooden shacks built on stilts to protect the buildings from flooding. Housing remains a critical problem in Guyana. Many homes lack adequate sanitation and electricity. Slums are common in Georgetown and around rural plantations. The government has accomplished little in the way of new housing construction, though it has publicized ambitious plans.

◉ Education

According to some sources, 98 percent of the Guyanese population is literate, or able to read and write. This is the highest literacy rate in South America. Even so, many of Guyana's schools are in disrepair and their books are outdated. Teachers sometimes leave to find higher-paying jobs in other countries. Primary education is compulsory (required by law). It is free for citizens between the ages of six and fourteen years old. About 440 primary schools, staffed by 4,000 teachers, accommodate nearly 114,000 pupils. Secondary education is available in almost 350 schools. About 76 percent of the primary school students go on to high school. This is a nearly 20 percent increase over the number of students attending high school at the end of the twentieth century.

Students attend class at the **University of Guyana.**

Fifteen technical institutes provide vocational education. Most students study engineering, construction, and related practical studies. Founded in 1962, the University of Guyana occupies two modern campuses, one in the Georgetown suburb of Turkeyen and another in the small town of Tain. The university has an enrollment of about five thousand students. It offers programs of study in the arts, natural and social sciences, agriculture, technology, education, business, and public administration.

Visit www.vgsbooks.com for links to websites with additional information about the University of Guyana. Link to photos of the two campuses and learn how students are involved in their community.

Health

In the early twenty-first century, the country's infant mortality rate of 54 deaths in every 1,000 live births was higher than the South American average of 46 per 1,000. The life expectancy figure of 65 years of age is among the lowest figures in South America. Both of these statistics are worse than average in South America.

Public health standards have improved somewhat throughout Guyana. Hospitals and other medical facilities work to improve health conditions in urban and rural areas. They also educate Guyanese about how to prevent malaria, yellow fever, and AIDS (acquired immunodeficiency syndrome), for example. AIDS breaks down the body's immune system so that the body cannot fight off infections. AIDS is caused by a virus known as HIV (human immunodeficiency virus). It is most often spread by body fluids exchanged through sex or intravenous drug use. AIDS is the leading cause of death among people ages twenty to forty-nine in Guyana. About 2.5 percent of Guyana's adult population is infected with HIV. Guyana's government is addressing the AIDS epidemic by increasing public education about the spread of the disease, by testing donated blood, and by encouraging early diagnosis.

Providing health-care services to Amerindians and others who live in remote communities is difficult. Health workers must get past poor roads, flooding, and difficult terrain to set up a health camp. In cases where pollution impacts health, such as when miners pollute the waterways with mercury, the health of entire communities can be at risk.

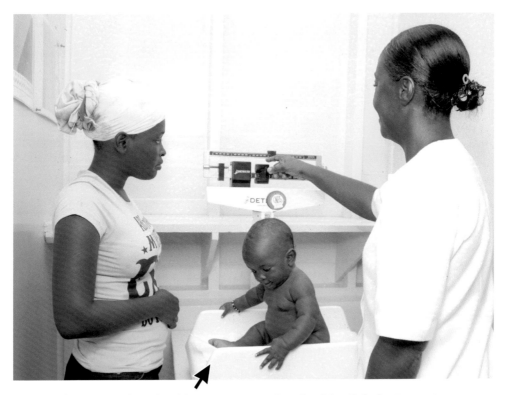

An infant receives health care at an urban health clinic in Georgetown. One of Guyana's **health-care challenges** is making health care accessible to people who live far from Guyana's major cities.

CULTURAL LIFE

Many Guyanese may be poor, but they enjoy a rich cultural heritage and close-knit communities. Storytelling, rhythmic music, and sports, as well as great art and literature, are a part of life in Guyana. Guyanese culture stems from many different influences, especially Caribbean, African, East Indian, European, and Amerindian.

Religion and Holidays

The Guyanese constitution guarantees religious freedom. During the 1800s, missionaries (religious leaders who travel to teach their religion) converted many Guyanese to Christianity. Most Guyanese of European, Chinese, Portuguese, and African heritage are Christians. Christians follow the teachings of Jesus. The main Christian branches are Pentacostalism, Roman Catholicism, and Anglicanism. About 17 percent of the population is Pentacostal, 8 percent is Roman Catholic, and 7 percent is Anglican. An additional 25 percent identifies itself as another branch of Christianity.

About 28 percent of Guyanese (mostly Indo-Guyanese) are Hindu. Hinduism is a religion that began in India about four thousand years ago. Traditionally, Hindus believe in many gods and goddesses. The caste system, which separates Hindus into professional and economic groups, does not exist in Guyana. And most Indo-Guyanese believe in only one god. A mandir, or Hindu temple, can be found in almost every Indo-Guyanese village.

In Guyana 7 percent of the population are Muslims, or people who follow the Islamic faith. Islam began on the Arabian Peninsula in the seventh century A.D. Its founder was the prophet Muhammad. Islam spread to southern Asia, which includes India. Most Muslims in Guyana are Indo-Guyanese.

Guyana's government observes all the major religious holidays of each of the three major faiths—Christian, Hindu, and Islam. Christmas (celebrating the birth of Jesus) and Easter (celebrating Jesus's rising from the dead) are the two biggest Christian celebrations in Guyana.

A couple is married in a traditional **Hindu wedding ceremony** in Guyana.

OBEAHISM

Obeah is a folk, or traditional, religion with roots in African and Christian belief systems. The government outlawed it because some practitioners seek to harm or control other people. However, Obeah priests also seek to help and heal people with folk magic. Among the tools of the Obeah practitioners are bones, blood, ashes, feathers, and old rags. People seek out Obeah priests to cure disease, to discover their enemies, to bring about success in love, to seek revenge, or to experience good luck in employment or financial dealings. The practices are common among both the African and East Indian populations, though Amerindians and some Europeans are also believers.

Hindus celebrate Diwali (the festival of lights) and Phagwah (the triumph of good over evil). The most important Islamic holiday is Ramadan. It commemorates Allah (God) sending teachings to Muhammad. During the month of Ramadan, Muslims do not eat between sunrise and sunset. At the end of the month, people celebrate with meals and gatherings.

The biggest and most colorful festival in Guyana is Mashramani. The name comes from an Amerindian word meaning "celebration of a job well done." Often called simply Mash, Mashramani celebrates the day that Guyana declared itself a republic, February 23, 1970. Costumes, parades, music, dancing, and good food all add to the color of the celebration.

The Arts

The visual arts in Guyana tend to reflect the country's ethnic diversity or to showcase the beauty of the rain forests. Stanley Greaves and Carl Anderson paint colorful Caribbean themes. Ronald Savory paints images of the rain forest. Aubrey Williams was born in Georgetown and later moved to Britain. But as an adult, the painter spent two years living with the Warao. During this time, Williams claimed to understand art for the first time. He based some of his work on ancient Amerindian rock engravings.

Amerindian art includes Warao handcrafted baskets. Using marsh reeds and fibers from palm trees, the Warao weave their baskets so tightly that they become stiff. Most of the baskets have lids and straps. The Warao use natural vegetable dyes to color some of the reeds.

Literature

Amerindian groups recite stories that have come down from ancient times. The stories are sometimes told through songs. Creation stories explain how a group came to be and are tied to a group's religious beliefs. Early Amerindians also drew extensive rock paintings and engravings to tell stories.

Guyana has long provided a theme for literary expression. Well-known novels relating to the Guyana region include Arthur Conan Doyle's *The Lost World* and William Henry Hudson's *Green Mansions*.

Many authors of popular works were born in Guyana but moved out of the country. These people include Wilson Harris, Jan Carew, Denis Williams, Christopher Nicole, and E. R. Braithwaite. Braithwaite's memoir *To Sir, with Love* details his experiences as a black high school teacher in a white London slum. The work was praised for its hopeful view of difficult race relations. It became the subject of a major motion picture in 1967.

Edgar Mittelholzer, a Guyanese of Swiss origin, is well known outside of his native country. He wrote novels including *Corentyne Thunder* and a three-part novel known as the Kaywana trilogy. The latter set of stories follows one family through 350 years of Guyana's history. *Miramy*, a full-length Guyanese comedy by Frank Pilgrim, is set on an imaginary island in the West Indies. It became the first locally written play to be performed overseas.

Film

Guyana is not typically known for film productions, but in 2004, it became the subject of a motion picture. Guyana-born Rohit Jagessar released *Guiana 1838*. The movie tells the story of Guyana's East Indian immigrants, who first arrived as indentured servants in 1838.

CRICKET

Cricket teams consist of eleven members, but the game's main action is between a bowler (pitcher) and a batsman (batter). The bowler throws the ball to the batsman, who attempts to hit it with the bat. If the player does and if the ball goes to the edge of or outside of the boundaries of the field, the player scores points, called runs. If the ball is caught, the player is considered out and is done batting. The player continues to bat until he or she has been called out—an event that can take hours to occur. Individual batting scores of one hundred runs (called centuries) are notable but not uncommon.

After all eleven batsmen have come to bat— which represents half of an inning—the teams switch activities to complete the inning. Because the teams each have two innings at bat, a cricket match can easily take more than a day to complete.

Jagessar, a music producer, wrote and directed the film. *Guiana 1838* was Jagessar's first film, and it won the Best Feature Film award at the third Belize International Film Festival.

▷ Sports and Recreation

Cricket and volleyball are the most popular team sports in Guyana. Cricket is a ball-and-bat sport that somewhat resembles baseball. It is played in Britain and throughout the former British colonial world—in Africa, India, and the West Indies—with great enthusiasm. In 2007 Guyana opened the Guyana National Stadium and hosted the 2007 Cricket World Cup. The sports facility seats fifteen thousand people and is the top cricket facility in the Caribbean. Schools, local groups, and professional clubs all organize volleyball teams.

Guyanese children play cricket in Georgetown.

Music

Guyana's music, like its art, is strongly influenced by the nation's various ethnic groups. It includes plenty of rhythm. Amerindians play folk music using drums and reed instruments. Their music is closely linked to the sounds of nature. *Shanto* is a form of folk music that is similar to calypso, a lighthearted tropical music first performed by African slaves in the Caribbean. Reggae (from Jamaica) and other forms of Latin American music are also popular in Guyana. Some of the most popular performers are Dave Martin & the Tradewinds, Eddy Grant, and Terry Gajraj.

For the 2007 Cricket World Cup, Guyanese calypso artist Terry Gajraj recorded a song called "Cricket, Lovely Cricket." You can see and hear the performance by visiting YouTube .com.

Instruments include the Caribbean steel drums, or pans. Made from the metal top of oil drums, these percussion instruments produce different tones when struck. Steel-drum players are called pannists. Sometimes dozens of pannists form a steel-drum band. Guyana even has a National Steel Orchestra.

Some of Guyana's music is political. In the 1950s, British composer Alan Bush wrote *Cane Reapers*, an opera celebrating how the Guyanese were resisting British rule.

Visit www.vgsbooks.com for links to websites with additional information about the culture of Guyana. Listen to samples of Guyana's traditional and contemporary music and follow Guyanese sports teams.

Food

Each of Guyana's ethnic groups has contributed foods that have become a regular part of Guyanese dining habits. English roast beef, puddings (desserts), and tea appear with Indian curries (spicy dishes) and Chinese coconut buns. Portuguese garlic pork (pork marinated in vinegar with garlic and spices) and African *metemgee* (vegetables, fish, meat, and dumplings cooked in coconut milk) are also popular dishes.

In rural areas, the diet is simpler than it is in urban regions. A rural family begins the day with a meal called tea. This light meal consists

Women sell fresh okra in the Georgetown market square.

of bread and margarine, sometimes accompanied by a brew made from the leaves of the soursop (a tropical fruit). Breakfast—the main meal of the day—is served at eleven thirty. It usually consists of rice, potatoes, and fish or meat. Suppertime is at five thirty or six and may include rice and bits of pork.

Left: Soursop fruit and leaves grow on trees in warm and humid climates.
Right: This bowl of metemgee contains plantains, a fruit grown in Guyana that is similar to bananas.

For thousands of years, Amerindians have used a sauce called *cassareep* to spice their food. Cassareep is a blend of cassava juice, salt, and pepper. Amerindians add cassareep to a simmering pot of potatoes, beans, and meat to make a dish called pepperpot. Pepperpot is still served throughout the Caribbean. And it can be eaten for breakfast, lunch, and dinner.

COCONUT BUNS

Coconut buns can be found in most kitchens throughout Guyana and the Caribbean. The recipe for coconut buns originated in China. The buns are almost like cookies and produce a sweet and delicate aroma when baking. Guyanese eat coconut buns at breakfast or as a snack.

2 cups all-purpose flour	2 eggs
1 cup white sugar	½ cup milk
1 teaspoon baking powder	1 teaspoon vanilla extract
½ teaspoon salt	½ teaspoon almond extract
1 cup butter, cut into pieces	¾ cup flaked coconut

1. Preheat the oven to 350°F (175°C).
2. In a large bowl, stir together the flour, sugar, baking powder, and salt.
3. Add the butter. Press and cut the butter pieces into the flour mixture, using the back side of a fork, until the mixture resembles fine crumbs.
4. In a separate bowl, whisk together the eggs, milk, vanilla extract, and almond extract.
5. Pour the wet ingredients into the bowl with the butter and dry ingredients. Add the coconut, and mix just enough to blend.
6. Drop by rounded tablespoonfuls onto ungreased cookie sheets.
7. Bake for 20 minutes in the preheated oven, or until golden brown.

THE ECONOMY

Guyana draws most of its wealth from its natural resources. The country's forests are rich in valuable hardwoods. Underground lie deposits of gold, diamonds, and bauxite, the raw material from which aluminum is made. In addition, sugarcane and rice thrive in Guyana's hot, wet climate.

At one time, Guyana had a balanced and well-tuned economy that depended upon agricultural products and mining resources. But after Guyana won its independence in the 1960s, the country experienced one of the fastest economic declines in modern history. The production of major exports—sugar, bauxite, and rice—fell, while inflation (rising prices) worsened. Payment of foreign debts claimed much of Guyana's export income. Thousands of workers emigrated from the country, and state-owned businesses experienced a shortage of skilled workers.

In the 1990s, the country's economic picture improved. The government lifted controls on prices, wages, and trade. It also sold state-owned businesses to private investors. Guyana's gross domestic

product (GDP)—the monetary value of all the goods and services a country produces within a year—rose sharply. Guyana, however, still faced a heavy foreign debt, a labor shortage, and falling production of important exports such as gold and bauxite. The country lacked important infrastructure, such as roads and port facilities. And it had yet to develop its fishing and forestry into successful export businesses.

The unemployment rate in Guyana is 9.1 percent, a typical rate for a South American country. In addition to unemployment, food shortages have reduced the quality of life in Guyana. Throughout the years, food shortages and unemployment have resulted in mass emigrations and waves of violent crime. Guyana is losing many of its skilled and unskilled laborers, who seek a safer life and better jobs elsewhere. As a result, the country suffers a shortage of skilled labor.

In the twenty-first century, Guyana's GDP comes from three main economic sectors—services (47 percent), agriculture (31 percent), and industry (22 percent).

> Some of Guyana's most popular ecotourists are bird-watchers. They come from all over the world to catch a sight of the unique and colorful bird species found in the rain forest. Approximately eight hundred different bird species can be found in Guyana.

◯ Services

In Guyana 48 percent of the work-force has jobs that offer some type of service. Doctors, accountants, teachers, government workers, and hotel clerks are some examples of service workers. These workers do not produce a product, such as a television set or a candy bar. They help people or businesses in one way or another.

Tourism is the service industry in Guyana with the most potential, especially ecotourism. Ecotourists seek to explore places that are undisturbed by civilization and that offer glimpses of rarely seen wildlife. As one of the few countries that still has millions of acres of pristine rain forests, Guyana is poised for ecotourism. Guyana's rain forest has the potential to attract thousands of tourists each year. But the nation needs to invest in more hotels and paved roads to make it easier for tourists to visit. In addition, most tourists want to feel safe when they travel. The fear of crime and violence related to ethnic tensions in the nation may prevent some ecotourists from visiting Guyana.

In the Iwokrama rain forest reserve, land managers, scientists, and Amerindians work together to determine how local communities and the country can profit from the rain forest. At the same time, they work to preserve its unique and varied plant and animal life. Most tourists in Guyana visit Iwokrama.

On the Demerara River, a load of **exotic woods** harvested from Guyana's rain forest is prepared for transport.

Preserving Guyana's rain forests has the potential to bring huge economic benefits to the country in other ways. In all, 40 million acres (16 million hectares) of rain forest cover Guyana. The world needs the tropical rain forests of South America. Trees absorb carbon dioxide, helping to reduce global warming. But when trees are cut down, they release all the carbon they've absorbed. Keeping the rain forests intact prevents extreme amounts of carbon dioxide from entering the atmosphere. President Bharrat Jagdeo believes that keeping Guyana's trees standing should be more profitable than cutting them down to make lumber and other wood products. He is pushing for the global community to compensate countries such as Guyana for the ecological service of maintaining rain forests so they continue to store and collect harmful greenhouse gases. Yet in early 2008, Jagdeo awarded a U.S. logging company the right to log 1 million acres (404.69 hectares) of Guyana's rain forest, arguing that his country needs the dollars generated from such deals.

The rain forest places Guyana in a powerful bargaining position. Critics argue that if enough companies do not step forward, Guyana can threaten to cut down its rain forests. This would contribute significantly to global warming. Jagdeo and other supporters argue that Guyana is offering a valuable service, and many people see Jagdeo as an environmental hero.

◉ Agriculture

That Arawak and other Amerindians developed about 60 percent of the crops that are still commonly grown in South America. Agriculture is important to Guyana's economy, although only 28 percent of the workforce is engaged in farming. The main cash crops include sugarcane—from which rum and molasses, as well as sugar, are derived—rice, coconuts, cassava, and mangoes. Production of sugarcane and rice, found mostly on the coastal plain, still requires much manual labor. Agricultural production increased in the middle of the twentieth century. But labor strikes, droughts, flooding, pests, and scant supplies of fertilizer and farm equipment frequently interfere with production.

Sugarcane is Guyana's major agricultural crop. Almost half of all farmworkers are employed in raising and harvesting sugarcane. In the early 1990s, this crop made up more than one-third of the value of Guyana's exports to foreign countries. In 2006 the European Union, a leading importer of sugarcane from the Caribbean, announced a 36 percent cut in the price it was willing to pay for the sweetener. Guyana received a loan to modernize its sugar-processing plants. The new equipment helps Guyana to process sugarcane more efficiently and also allows for diversification, such as producing ethanol (fuel made from crops high in sugar) and other sugar by-products.

Sugarcane cultivation is confined almost exclusively to a belt of land varying in width from 2 to 8 miles (3 to 13 km) along the coastal plain between the Courantyne and Essequibo rivers. The typical plantation has an ocean frontage protected by a seawall. The first mile from the sea may be used for growing rice or for pasture. Farther inland, for distances of up to 8 miles, the land is used to grow sugarcane.

Indentured plantation workers introduced rice production to Guyana. By the last decade of the nineteenth century, the grain had become an important commercial crop. Rice is Guyana's second-most-important agricultural product. During a normal year, Guyanese harvest more than 300,000 tons (272,000 metric tons) of rice. It is both the staple foodstuff of the country and an export product that generates just under 8 percent of the export revenues. Small-scale farmers plant over 250,000 acres (101,171 hectares) of rice paddies. Most of these farms are less than 5 acres (2 hectares) in size. Nearly one-third of the total population depends upon rice cultivation for a living.

Rice farms are highly mechanized, with combines and tractors replacing hand tools and oxen. To prevent the growth of weeds, farmers flood the rice paddies with water that comes from reservoirs. The water travels to the paddies by way of an intricate network of irrigation canals. The canals are lined with a heavy clay soil that prevents water from seeping through.

Planting occurs at the beginning of the long rainy season in April or

FLOOD FALLOWING

In the mid-1800s, Guyanese farmers developed flood fallowing, a method of growing sugarcane that farmers still use. Workers till the fields and then flood them for at least six months. Then the farmers drain the fields before planting the sugarcane. Once planted, sugarcane grows for twelve to eighteen months before reaching maturity. When the crop is ready for harvest, field-workers set the 12-foot (4 m) stalks on fire so that they can be cut by hand more easily. After piling the stalks in rows, workers transport them to mills on flat-bottomed barges. Oxen, mules, or tractors tow the watercraft along canals.

The root-stubble that remains in the ground produces new shoots called rations. After five years, the land begins to yield fewer shoots, and the flood-fallowing process begins again. Flood fallowing increases yields by as much as 40 percent.

Workers in Guyana **harvest rice** using a combine harvester.

May, and the harvest takes place during the dry month of October. In areas with extremely good soil, two crops may be grown each year. The best lands produce up to 2,000 pounds (907 kg) of rice per acre, and the average throughout the country ranges from 60 to 75 percent of that figure.

Inaccessible pastureland hinders the growth of Guyana's livestock industry. In addition, the savanna's native grasses have low nutritional value. Periodic outbreaks of hoof-and-mouth disease (HMD) have occurred. HMD is a highly contagious virus that causes a fever and blisters in the mouth and feet of hoofed animals. Ranchers usually destroy the infected animals before they spread the disease. Vampire bats have transmitted rabies to the livestock. Consequently, beef production is barely sufficient to supply local needs.

The prospects for raising livestock are getting better. Ranchers have brought in hardy breeds, such as Santa Gertrudis and zebu, that resist hoof-and-mouth disease. The planting of more nutritious, imported grasses has also contributed to the growth in this segment of the economy. About 110,000 cattle and 130,000 sheep feed on pasturelands, mostly in the Rupununi Savanna.

Even though it borders the Atlantic Ocean, Guyana has not developed its fishing industry. The fish that are caught are sold locally. Shrimp is the exception. Guyana started developing its shrimp industry in the 1980s. In the early twenty-first century, shrimp trawlers and shrimp farms are common sights.

Pirates still operate in Caribbean waters. In the early twenty-first century, Guyana cracked down on Guyanese pirates who attack fishing vessels and shrimp trawlers. Armed with guns, the pirates steal fish and shrimp catches, money, fuel, other valuables, and sometimes even small vessels.

The timber industry is based upon the logging of valuable woods found within the rain forests. Loggers encounter a number of difficulties in the cutting and transporting of timber, including inadequate roads in the forested areas. Other difficulties include the absence of uniform rules for grading the lumber, inadequate mills, and the shortage of shipping and storage space for exporters.

The major market demand has been for greenheart, a wood famous for its resistance to termites and decay. Areas bordering rivers have been heavily exploited. To preserve the rain forests, Guyana suspended many logging permits, and by 2007, logging in Guyana had decreased by more than 16 percent.

Industry

Manufacturing, mining, and other industrial jobs employ about 24 percent of Guyana's workforce. Bauxite replaced sugar as Guyana's leading export in the 1970s. Bauxite production, which began in 1914,

The view of a **bauxite plant** in Guyana. Most bauxite is processed into aluminum.

This aerial view of the **Omai gold mines** shows the chemical waste spilled over from the broken retaining wall in the holding pond.

totaled 1.8 million tons (1.6 million metric tons) in 2005. Guyana is one of the world's leading producers of this ore. Even so, bauxite production has fallen dramatically in recent years. Guyana faces stiff competition and lower prices from other bauxite-producing countries. More than 90 percent of Guyana's annual bauxite production comes from the Linden region, about 70 miles (113 km) up the Demerara River. To mine bauxite, workers remove a thick layer of white sand and clay from the ground and extract the ore from the exposed surface.

Even though El Dorado proved to be only a Spanish legend, gems and precious minerals such as gold have contributed substantially to the country's wealth. In 2002 gold made up 27.5 percent of Guyana's exports, making it the leading export. But by 2005, the Omai mine, which produced about 70 percent of Guyana's gold, was nearly depleted of the mineral. Gold remains only in the inaccessible parts of the mine. Smaller gold mining sites have been located in Guyana.

Guyana's need for the revenues it earns from gold may need to be balanced with the environmental risks of mining. In August 1995, a spill at a gold-mining site emptied 3.5 million tons (3.2 million metric tons) of cyanide-laced water into a tributary of the Essequibo River. As a result, the government temporarily shut down gold production to review environmental conditions at the site. The government has spent hundreds of millions of dollars to clean up the site. The spill contaminated drinking water, killed wildlife, and raised various health concerns in many Amerindian communities.

Guyana has three television stations but only about forty-six thousand television sets. The government runs one station and controls the content of the news. Two other stations are satellite and can be viewed in the United States. They feature news, sports, and entertainment. About one-third of the population owns a cell phone. One-quarter of the population has an Internet connection, and most people have radios.

Energy

Guyana gets most of its energy from imported oil. To lessen its dependence on high-priced oil, Guyana is developing its waterpower. The Amaila Falls Hydroelectric Project is located on the Kuribrong River, a tributary of the Potaro River in west central Guyana. The plant will harness the power of the waterfalls to generate electricity for the entire nation. The plant will use the waterfalls to spin the blades of a giant turbine, or an engine that extracts energy from a fluid such as water. The turbine is connected to a generator, a device that converts the mechanical energy of the waterfalls into electricity. Hydroelectric plants are one of the cleanest and cheapest sources of electricity.

The floor of Guyana's ocean waters contains an estimated 15 billion barrels of oil. Since the maritime boundary dispute with Suriname was settled in 2007, Guyana has the right to drill in the oil-rich seabed. Further investment is needed to explore this source of revenue.

Visit www.vgsbooks.com for links to websites with additional information about Guyana's natural resources and plans for the future of its industries.

The Future

In 2008 Guyana joined other Caribbean countries and the European Union in signing an Economic Partnership Agreement (EPA). The trade agreement will over time eliminate most of the duties (charges) and quotas that governments place on exports and imports. Guyana hopes the agreement will allow it to develop new exports. Those who are against the EPA say that the agreement will force Guyana and other Caribbean nations to raise taxes to replace income lost from lower pricing and absent duties.

Free and fair elections are a sign that political reforms are in place and working. But the economy has a long way to go. Industrial development depends on a reliable power supply. Guyana's energy sources are overtaxed by aging equipment. Sometimes the power

Because much of Guyana's wealth lies in its **natural resources,** it is important that the country continue to find ways to protect its resources.

plants shut down for most of the day, forcing factories to close for the day. Retooling factories with modern equipment is necessary to keep Guyana competitive in the agricultural and mining sectors.

Another issue is Venezuela's claim to the Essequibo region, which comprises more than two-thirds of Guyana. In addition, Guyana's ethnic tensions still run high. A strongly united population would help the Guyanese deal with poverty and crime.

President Jagdeo's work in reforming the economy has attracted more foreign investment. This may eventually help to create more jobs and a workforce that chooses to stay in the country. Guyana's natural resources, especially its vast rain forest and undeveloped waterpower, can help to make the nation a leader in environmental progress.

3500 B.C..	Warao and Arawak first live in what later becomes Guyana. They hunt, fish, and gather shellfish and fruit for food.
1000 B.C.	Arawak begin planting cassava and corn.
A.D. 1300s	Caribs arrive in Guyana from southern South America.
1498	Christopher Columbus sails along the coast of Guyana.
1499	Spanish explorer Alonso de Ojeda becomes the first European to set foot on Guyana.
1593	Pedro da Silva heads an ill-fated expedition to Guyana to search for the mythical El Dorado.
1595-1616	Walter Raleigh of England leads three expeditions to Guyana and maps the coastline.
1616	Dutch colonists establish Kyk-Over-al, the first permanent Dutch settlement in Guyana.
1621	The Dutch West India Company is granted authority over Guyana and the right to import slaves from Africa.
1742	Laurens Storm van's Gravesande encourages colonial movement from the interior to the coast.
1763	During Cuffy's Revolt, slaves overtake plantations, killing four thousand slave owners and their families.
1770s	More than fifteen thousand slaves toil in Guyana.
1781	The British win Guyana in a war against the Dutch.
1782-84	The French take over Guyana and establish the town of Longchamps.
1784	The Dutch regain power and make Longchamps the colonial capital and rename it Stabroek (later Georgetown).
1796	The British conquer Guyana.
1800	Slaves number one hundred thousand.
1802	The Dutch regain control of Guyana under the Treaty of Amiens.
1803	The British again conquer Guyana.
1807	Britain begins the process of abolishing the slave trade throughout the British Empire, including Guyana.
1814	Under the Treaty of Paris, the British are officially awarded Guyana, which they name British Guiana. The Dutch take over Dutch Guiana (present-day Suriname), and the French secure French Guiana.

1834 Slavery is abolished in all British colonies, including Guyana.

1850 Only 916 of a population of 130,000 are eligible to vote.

1917 The indenture system is abolished in British Guiana.

1940 Political parties are legalized.

1945 Women are allowed to vote.

1950 Forbes Burnham and Cheddi Jagan cofound the People's Progressive Party (PPP).

1957 Forbes Burnham forms the People's National Congress (PNC).

1961 The election of Cheddi Jagan sparks rioting in Georgetown.

1962 The University of Guyana is founded.

1966 Guyana achieves independence from Britain.

1967 Guyanese author E. R. Braithwaite's novel *To Sir, with Love* becomes a major motion picture starring Sidney Poitier.

1970 Guyana establishes the Cooperative Republic of Guyana.

1978 Jonestown is the site of a mass suicide.

1980 The new constitution declares that a president, not the prime minister, heads the government.

1980s Guyana replaces Haiti as the poorest nation in Latin America.

1985 President Forbes Burnham dies. Hugh Desmond Hoyte assumes office.

1989 The Guyana government creates the Iwokrama International Centre for Rain Forest Conservation and Development.

1992 Cheddi Jagan is elected president.

1995 A gold-mining accident poisons a tributary of the Essequibo River.

1997 Janet Jagan becomes the first woman president of Guyana.

1999 Janet Jagan resigns. Prime Minister Bharrat Jagdeo assumes office.

2001 Bharrat Jagdeo is elected president.

2006 In the first peaceful election in twenty years, Jagdeo is reelected.

2007 The United Nations settles Guyana's maritime boundary dispute with Suriname. Guyana hosts the Cricket World Cup.

2008 Guyana signs the Economic Partnership Agreement (EPA) with the European Union (EU).

COUNTRY NAME Cooperative Republic of Guyana

AREA 83,000 square miles (214,969 sq. km)

MAIN LANDFORMS coastal plain, sand and clay region, Rupununi Savanna, Pakaraima Mountains, Serra Acaraí, Kanuku Mountains

HIGHEST POINT Mount Roraima, 9,094 feet (2,772 m) above sea level

LOWEST POINT 10 feet (3 m) below sea level along the coast

MAJOR RIVERS Essequibo, Courantyne, Demerara, Berbice, Cuyuni

ANIMALS anteaters, Antillean manatees, arapaima, bushmasters, caimans, capybaras, deer, ducks, herons, himeralli, howler monkeys, ibis, jaguars, kingfishers, labarria, macaws, peccaries, piranhas, plovers, snipes, spider monkeys, tapirs, vampire bats

CAPITAL CITY Georgetown

OTHER MAJOR CITIES Linden, New Amsterdam

OFFICIAL LANGUAGE English

MONETARY UNIT Guyanese dollar. 100 cents = 1 dollar.

GUYANESE CURRENCY

Guyana's central bank, the Bank of Guyana, was established in 1965, just a year before Guyana achieved independence from Britain. Upon independence in 1966, the Guyanese dollar (GYD) replaced the East Caribbean dollar in Guyana. Coins are issued in denominations of $1, $5, and $10 (the cent is no longer used because of inflation). Rice harvest, sugarcane, and gold mining are pictured on each coin, respectively. Banknotes are $5, $100, $500, and $1,000.

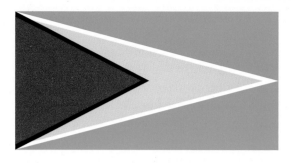

Dr. Whitney Smith, a U.S. flag designer, designed the Guyanese flag in 1962. Guyana adopted the flag in 1966 upon independence. The green stands for Guyana's forests and agriculture. The golden arrowhead symbolizes the nation's mineral wealth and its rich future. The red triangle represents the country's eagerness to build a strong independent nation. The white and black lines were not in Smith's original design but were added later. The white symbolizes water. The black stands for the strength and endurance of Guyana's people.

Robert Cyril Gladstone Potter and Archibald Leonard Luker wrote the music and words to Guyana's national song. Guyana adopted the anthem in 1966.

Dear land of Guyana, of rivers and plains,
Made rich by the sunshine, and lush by the rains.
Set gem-like and fair, between mountains and sea,
Your children salute you, dear land of the free.

Green land of Guyana, our heroes of yore,
Both bondsmen and free, laid their bones on your shore.
This soil so they hallowed, and from them are we,
All sons of one mother, Guyana the free.

Great land of Guyana, diverse though our strains,
We are born of their sacrifice, heirs of their pains.
And ours is the glory their eyes did not see,
One land of six peoples, united and free.

Dear land of Guyana, to you will we give,
Our homage, our service, each day that we live.
God guard you, Great Mother, and make us to be
More worthy our heritage, land of the free.

For a link to a site where you can listen to Guyana's national anthem, visit www.vgsbooks.com.

EDWARD RICARDO (E. R.) BRAITHWAITE (b. 1920) Braithwaite is a Guyanese writer, teacher, and diplomat. He was born in Georgetown and is best known for his stories of social conditions and racial discrimination against black people. During World War II, he joined the Royal Air Force in Great Britain as a pilot. He later earned a doctorate in physics from the University of Cambridge. After the war, Braithwaite could not find work in his area so he began teaching in London. He based the book *To Sir, with Love* (1959) on his experiences.

FORBES BURNHAM (1923–1985) Linden Forbes Sampson Burnham was born in Kitty, a suburb of Georgetown. An excellent student, he went to Queen's College in Georgetown and won a scholarship to attend the University of London in 1942. Burnham studied law and returned to Guyana in 1949 as a moderate Socialist. He cofounded the People's Progressive Party, which won the first elections held in British Guiana in 1953. In 1966 Burnham led Guyana to be a nation independent from Britain and became Guyana's first prime minister. In 1970 Burnham became president and declared Guyana a Socialist government. He established strong relations with Cuba, the Soviet Union, and other Communist countries. He died suddenly in 1985.

SHAKIRA BAKSH CAINE (b. 1947) A Guyanese of East Indian descent, Shakira Baksh was a model and actress when actor Michael Caine saw her in a commercial and was drawn to her beauty. The two married in 1973 and have one daughter. Shakira Caine appeared in the movie *The Man Who Would Be King*.

CUFFY (d. 1763) A slave from western Africa, Cuffy is remembered as a national hero of Guyana for leading twenty-five hundred slaves into a revolt against slavery in 1763. Cuffy was a slave at a cooperage (a place that makes barrels) at Plantation Lilienburg. He and his army of slaves overthrew the governor of the district of Berbice before government forces subdued them. Cuffy killed himself after losing a battle with Akara, another slave leader in the rebellion.

DESREY FOX (b. 1955) is a minister in Guyana's Ministry of Education. Fox was born in a small Amerindian village called Waramadong, in the upper Mazarin district of western Guyana. She worked as a nurse in Georgetown but quit partly because she found it hard to adapt to the schedules and rules of Western society. Later, feeling as if she'd failed her people, she took a job as a researcher at the University of Guyana, where she compiled a dictionary of an ancient Amerindian language. In her role as minister, Fox is responsible for making sure Amerindian children living in remote areas receive an education and become eligible for scholarships. She continues to emphasize the need to preserve Guyana's ancient and dying Amerindian languages.

EDMUND MONTAGUE (EDDY) GRANT (b. 1948) This musician was born in Plaisance, Guyana, and moved with his family to Great Britain as a young child. Grant performs a style of music called soca, a blend of soul, calypso, and African rhythms. His lengthy career took off in 1968 with the hit song "Baby Come Back," performed with the Equals. Later solo hits include "Electric Avenue" (1983). Grant runs his own recording company in the Caribbean nation of Barbados.

JANET JAGAN (1920–2009) In 1997 Jagan was elected president of Guyana. She became Guyana's first female president. Jagan was born Janet Rosenberg in Chicago, Illinois, to a middle-class Jewish family. She worked as a student nurse in Chicago's Cook County Hospital, where she met Cheddi Jagan, an Indo-Guyanese dentistry student. The two married in 1943 and moved to Guyana. The couple got involved in politics. In 1953 Janet was elected to the House of Assembly. Janet resigned from the presidency in 1999 because of failing health. She became editor of *Thunder*, a PPP publication. To ensure that Guyanese children see themselves in the books they read, Jagan wrote several children's books, including *When Grandpa Cheddi Was a Boy and Other Stories*.

CLIVE LLOYD (b. 1944) Born in Georgetown, Lloyd made sports history as one of the most successful captains in West Indies cricket. Nicknamed Supercat for his ability to leap stealthily into action, Lloyd was an excellent fielder and batter. During his ten years as captain in the 1970s and 1980s, his team lost only two out of eighteen series and won two out of three World Cups.

GRACE NICHOLS (b. 1950) An award-winning poet from Georgetown, Nichols writes for adults and children in Caribbean rhythms. Her topics include Caribbean culture and Guyanese and Amerindian folklore.

WALTER RODNEY (1942–1980) Rodney, a prominent Guyanese historian and political figure, was born to a working-class family in Georgetown. While teaching in Jamaica in 1968, the government banned him from the country because of his support of the poor. Rioting broke out and is remembered in his honor as the Rodney Riots. In 1974 Rodney returned to Guyana from a teaching position in Tanzania, Africa. He became increasingly active in politics. In 1980 Rodney was killed in a bomb explosion while running for office.

GEORGETOWN Guyana's capital city offers a variety of interesting places to visit. The Guyana National Museum, established in 1868, exhibits materials related to Guyana's wildlife and cultural heritage. The Parliament Building is where Guyana's government meets. Completed in 1834, it is one of only two domed buildings in Guyana. The Parliament Building is also the place where Guyana's freed slaves were allowed to purchase land for the first time. Saint George's Cathedral is the tallest wooden structure in South America. On the Atlantic Coast in Georgetown, visitors can walk along the long seawall constructed to protect the city from flooding. The bandstand along the seawall is a center of activity, where city dwellers go to enjoy the ocean breeze, fly a kite, and order food from one of the many vendors. Stabroek Market is the city's lively marketplace. Built in 1881, it covers an area of about 80,000 square feet (7,000 sq. m). The building sits on land and over water. It houses vendors selling everything from fruits to furniture and gold.

IWOKRAMA INTERNATIONAL CENTRE FOR RAIN FOREST CONSERVATION AND DEVELOPMENT The center manages about 1 million acres (371,000 hectares) of rain forest in central Guyana and researches how to use the natural resources to provide ecological, social, and economic benefits locally and worldwide. At Iwokrama visitors can tour the rain forest and see tropical plants and animals in their natural habitat.

KAIETEUR FALLS Tucked away in the jungles of west central Guyana, Kaieteur Falls is considered one of the most spectacular waterfalls in the world. It can be reached by plane or by trekking for three to five days on a wilderness trail. The water drops 741 feet (226 m), and visitors can see many endangered animal and plant species from the nature walk.

KYK-OVER-AL See the four-hundred-year-old remains of the original Dutch fort built in 1616. Little is left of the fort, but visitors can walk through the ruins and imagine Guyana defending itself from British and French attacks.

SANTA MISSION Santa Mission is a small Amerindian village on the banks of Pokerero Creek in central Guyana. Visitors can canoe, look for exotic wildlife such as caiman and colorful birds, and shop for handcrafted Amerindian items.

SHELL BEACH Located on the Atlantic coast near the Venezuela border, Shell Beach is known for its white sands and its protected turtle population. Four out of eight sea turtle species nest on the beach.

bauxite: a sedimentary rock that is an aluminum ore. Bauxite is stripped from the surface of open pit mines. When water is removed from the ore, a white powder (aluminum oxide) remains and is used to make aluminum.

carbon dioxide: a gas (CO_2) that concentrates naturally in Earth's atmosphere. Plants absorb carbon dioxide when growing in the spring and summer and release carbon dioxide when dying in the fall and winter. Humans have increased carbon dioxide emissions by burning fossil fuels that contain carbon, such as oil and coal.

debt relief: the forgiveness of debts built up by low-income countries and owed to wealthy nations

global warming: the increase of the average temperature of Earth's air and oceans, measured since the mid-twentieth century

greenhouse gas: several gases that line Earth's atmosphere, absorbing and emitting radiation from Earth's surface. Without greenhouse gases, Earth's temperature would be so cold it would be uninhabitable. A buildup of greenhouse gases, caused by pollution and deforestation, works to warm Earth's temperature. Greenhouse gases include water vapor, carbon dioxide, methane, nitrous oxide, and ozone.

People's National Congress (PNC): founded in 1957 by Forbes Burnham, the PNC dominated Guyana politics from 1964 through 1992, in part by rigging elections. A Socialist party, the PNC was in power when Guyana gained independence in 1966. Over the next thirty years, the government absorbed many of Guyana's private businesses and led the nation into economic decline.

People's Progressive Party (PPP): Guyana's first modern political party, the PPP was founded by Cheddi Jagan (an East Indian Communist) and Forbes Burnham (an African Socialist) in 1950. By uniting races, the leaders hoped to push for Guyana's independence from Britain. The PPP won the 1953 election, but the government lasted only 133 days. Forbes Burnham later split from the PPP to form the People's National Congress. Britain interfered, accusing the leaders of leading the country to Communism. The PPP has been in power since 1992 and has abandoned some of its Communist practices in order to stimulate the economy.

poldering: artificially draining an area of river, lake, or seawater to expose an area of land rich in nutrients and good for farming. The land is protected from reflooding by the building of a dike, or earthen wall.

Socialism: a set of economic principles that advocate collective ownership of businesses, resulting in a society where wealth is distributed more evenly, lessening the divide between rich and poor

soursop: fruit from a flowering evergreen tree that grows in the West Indies and Latin America. It is difficult to eat and is usually juiced.

Glossary

Ameringer, Charles D., ed. *Political Parties of the Americas, 1980s to 1990s: Canada, Latin America, and the West Indies*. Westport, CT: Greenwood Publishing Group, 1992.
This scholarly publication provides an in-depth look at the motives and histories of the political parties of Guyana and other countries in the Western Hemisphere.

"The Arawak." N.d.
http://www.pages.drexel.edu/~sd65/carib_history/Arawaks.htm (January 27, 2008).
This article describes the pre-Columbian culture of the Amerindians known as Arawak.

BBC News. "Country Profile: Guyana." *BBC News*. 2009.
http://news.bbc.co.uk/2/hi/americas/country_profiles/1211325.stm (February 10, 2009).
The BBC is a source for comprehensive news coverage about Guyana and provides a country profile.

"The Caribs." N.d.
http://www.pages.drexel.edu/~sd65/carib_history/caribs.htm (January 27, 2008).
This article describes the pre-Columbian culture of the Amerindians known as Caribs.

Central Intelligence Agency (CIA). "Guyana." *The World Factbook*. 2009.
https://www.cia.gov/library/publications/the-world-factbook/print/gy.html (February 6, 2009).
This CIA website provides facts and figures on Guyana's geography, people, government, economy, communications, transportation, military, and more.

Economist. 2008.
http://www.economist.com/world/americas (November 12, 2008).
The on-line version of the *Economist*, a news magazine, is updated throughout the day, every day. The *Economist* is a source for comprehensive news coverage about Guyana and other countries.

Government of Guyana. "HIV/AIDS in Guyana." *National HIV/AIDS Programme*. January 25, 2008.
http://www.hiv.gov.gy/gp_hiv_gy.php (February 4, 2009).
The site offers in-depth coverage of the HIV/AIDS problem in Guyana, including details about prevention, education, and statistics, and includes a youth section.

International Human Rights Clinic, Human Rights Program. *All That Glitters: Gold Mining in Guyana*. Cambridge, MA: Harvard Law School, March 2007.
http://www.law.harvard.edu/programs/hrp/documents/AllThatGlitters.pdf (January 26, 2009).
The report details the harmful effects of mining on the environment and on Amerindian communities.

Mintz, Sidney. *Sweetness and Power: The Place of Sugar in Modern History*.
Mintz takes a look at the history of sugar consumption and how sugar plantations in the Caribbean helped to shape capitalism.

Population Reference Bureau. 2008.
http://www.prb.org (November 2008).
PRB provides annual, in-depth demographics on Guyana's population. It includes rates of birth, death, and infant mortality and other statistics relating to health, environment, education, employment, family planning, and more. Special articles cover environmental and health issues.

Ramraj, Robert. *Guyana: Population, Environments, Economic Activities.* Greensboro, NC: Battleground Printing and Publishing, 2003.
Ramraj provides a scholarly, comprehensive study of Guyana.

Turner, Barry, ed. *The Statesman's Yearbook 2009: The Politics, Cultures and Economies of the World.* New York: Macmillan Publishers, 2008.
The *Yearbook* provides a summary of Guyana's economy, culture, government, and more.

U.S. Department of State Bureau of Western Hemisphere Affairs. *Country Profiles.* July 2008.
http://www.state.gov/r/pa/ei/bgn/1984.htm (November 12, 2008).
Profiles of countries, including Guyana, produced by the U.S. Department of State are available at this site. Profiles include brief summaries of geography, people, government and politics, and economy.

Vereecke, Jorg. *National Report on Indigenous Peoples and Development.* United Nations Development Programme. Country Office: Guyana, December 1994.
http://www.sdnp.org.gy/undp-docs/nripd/ (January 26, 2009).
This report profiles the different Amerindian groups in Guyana. It provides their locations and describes health, education, political, and economic conditions.

Further Reading and Websites

Bootman, Colin. *The Steel Pan Man of Harlem*. Minneapolis: Carolrhoda Books, 2009.
This beautifully illustrated book retells the story of the Pied Piper of Hamelin with a Caribbean twist and a magical steel pan drum.

Campbell, Kumari. *United Kingdom in Pictures*. Minneapolis: Twenty-First Century Books, 2004.
This book in the Visual Geography Series® introduces readers to the United Kingdom, which played an important role in Guyana's history.

Caribbean Amerindian Centrelink
http://www.centrelink.org/index.html
This site provides information on the history, culture, and contemporary communities of indigenous peoples of the Caribbean, from the Guyanese to Central America and from the Antilles to North America.

Carnegie School of Home Economics. *What's Cooking in Guyana*. Oxford, UK: Macmillan Caribbean, 2004.
A collection of recipes common in Guyana and from various ethnic backgrounds, including Amerindian dishes, is available in this book.

Carter, Martin. *Poems by Martin Carter*. Oxford, UK: Macmillan Caribbean, 2006.
Carter wrote a collection of poems while in jail as a young Socialist in British Guiana.

Engfer, Lee. *India in Pictures*. Minneapolis: Twenty-First Century Books, 2003.
This title in the Visual Geography Series® gives the reader a comprehensive introduction to India. Read more about the country that contributed greatly to Guyana's history and culture.

Guyana Chronicle Online
http://www.guyanachronicle.com/
Read Guyana's government-run daily newspaper.

Hyde, Margaret O., and Emily G. Hyde. *World Religions 101: An Overview for Teens*. Minneapolis: Twenty-First Century Books, 2009.
Learn more about the major religions of the world, including Hinduism, Christianity, and Islam, in this book.

Ishmael, Odeen. *Amerindian Legends of Guyana*. Stevens Point, WI: Artex Publishing, Inc., 1995.
This book includes twenty Amerindian stories that reveal the history behind some Amerindian myths, traditions, and folklore.

Lace, William W. *The British Empire: The End of Colonialism*. Farmington Hills, MI: Lucent Books, 2000.
From History's Great Defeats series, this book describes the rise and fall of the largest colonial power in history.

McDonald, Ian. *The Humming-Bird Tree*. Oxford, UK: Macmillan Caribbean, 2004.
The book is a fictional account of race and class in Guyana from a young boy's view.

Mongabay.com
http://kids.mongabay.com/
Learn all about the many plants and animals of the rain forests, why they are disappearing, and how people can save them.

Morrison, Marion. *Guyana*. New York: Children's Press, 2003.
From the Enchantment of the World series, this book covers the cultural geography of Guyana.

Parnell, Helga. *Cooking the South American Way*. Minneapolis: Lerner Publications Company, 2003.
This cookbook features recipes from a variety of South American regions and gives additional information on the continent's traditions and foods.

Singh, B. R. *Birds of Guyana*. Oxford, UK: Macmillan Caribbean, 2004.
Singh offers detailed information about some of Guyana's most interesting bird species, along with a map showing where the birds can be found.

Stabroek News
http://www.stabroeknews.com/
Read the on-line publication of Guyana's leading privately owned daily newspaper.

Stephenson, Denise. *Dear People: Remembering Jonestown*. Berkeley, CA: Heyday Books, 2005.
Through letters and other original documents, the author tells the story of the rise and fall of the People's Temple, a California-based religious cult that came to a tragic end in Guyana.

vgsbooks.com
http://www.vgsbooks.com
Visit vgsbooks.com, the homepage of the Visual Geography Series®. You can get linked to all sorts of useful on-line information, including geographical, historical, demographic, cultural, and economic websites. The vgsbooks.com site is a great resource for late-breaking news and statistics.

Warao Indians of Venezuela
http://www.dolsenmusic.net/advocacy/case_study_1.html
Although this website is about the Warao of Venezuela, much of the information also applies to the nearby Warao of Guyana. Listen to the recordings of Warao lullabies, drums, and a shaman (priest) working to cure an illness.

Welsbacher, Anne. *Protecting Earth's Rain Forests*. Minneapolis: Lerner Publications Company, 2009.
Rain forests house important natural resources for Guyana and countries worldwide. Learn more about rain forests and the necessity of preserving them.

Captions for photos appearing on cover and chapter openers:

Cover: The national flower of Guyana is the *Victoria Amazonica*. The Amazonica is a water lily that can grow to more than 8 feet (2.4 m) across.

pp. 4–5 The Essequibo River valley in northwestern Guyana includes large areas of dense rain forest.

pp. 8–9 Foothills in the interior highlands run along the Pacaraima Mountain range.

pp. 38–39 People gather to celebrate Republic Day in Georgetown. Republic Day, also called Mashramani, commemorates the date on which Guyana became a republic.

pp. 46–47 Two girls giggle while enjoying their lunch.

pp. 54–55 A man prepares bundles of sugarcane to be loaded onto a punt, or boat, and carried down the canal.

Photo Acknowledgments

The images in this book are used with the permission of: © Dwayne Hackett, pp. 4–5, 8–9, 13, 14–15, 16, 19, 36, 38–39, 42, 43, 44, 45, 48, 52 (bottom right), 60, 62–63, 65; © XNR Productions, pp. 6, 10; © Duncan Simpson/ Panos Pictures, pp. 11, 54–55, 59; © Bill Curtsinger/National Geographic/ Getty Images, p. 12; © Mary Evans Picture Library/The Image Works, pp. 22, 25; © Mansell/Time & Life Pictures/Getty Images, p. 23; © Heiner Heine/ Imagebroker/Photolibrary, pp. 26, 40, 41, 46–47, 52 (top), 56; © Hulton Archive/Getty Images, p. 28; © Popperfoto/Getty Images, p. 29; AP Photo, p. 31; © Bob Henriques/Time & Life Pictures/Getty Images, p. 32; © Don Hogan Charles/Hulton Archive/Getty Images, p. 33; © Cynthia Johnson/Time & Life Pictures/Getty Images, p. 34 (top left); AP Photo/Ricardo Mazalan, p. 34 (top right); © Joe Corrigan/Getty Images, p. 34 (bottom); © Prakash Singh/AFP/ Getty Images, p. 50; © DEA/C. DANI-I. JESKE/Getty Images, p. 52 (bottom left); AP Photo/Jose Caruci, p. 61; Image courtesy of Banknotes.com - Audrius Tomonis, p. 68, © Laura Westlund/Independent Picture Service, p. 69.

Front cover: © John Warburton-Lee Photography/Photolibrary. Back cover: NASA.

AUG 2010